SURPRISED BY JOY

WISING UP ANTHOLOGIES

ILLNESS & GRACE, TERROR & TRANSFORMATION

FAMILIES: *The Frontline of Pluralism*

LOVE AFTER 70

DOUBLE LIVES, REINVENTION & THOSE WE LEAVE BEHIND

VIEW FROM THE BED: VIEW FROM THE BEDSIDE

SHIFTING BALANCE SHEETS:
Women's Stories Of Naturalized Citizenship & Cultural Attachment

COMPLEX ALLEGIANCES:
Constellations of Immigration, Citizenship, & Belonging

DARING TO REPAIR:
What Is It, Who Does It & Why?

CONNECTED:
What Remains As We All Change

CREATIVITY & CONSTRAINT

SIBLINGS: *Our First Macrocosm*

THE KINDNESS OF STRANGERS

SURPRISED BY JOY

A WISING UP ANTHOLOGY

Charles D. Brockett & Heather Tosteson
Editors

Wising Up Press

Wising Up Press
P.O. Box 2122
Decatur, GA 30031-2122
www.universaltable.org

Catalogue-in-Publication data is on file with the Library of Congress.
LCCN: 2018908040

Wising Up ISBN: 978-1-7324514-0-7

DEDICATION

To the memory of
Joyce Hamm Brockett
and
Dilys Bodycombe Tosteson
whose joy-filled souls shaped our lives

CONTENTS

III. FAMILY

IV. INTIMACY

V. THE QUOTIDIAN

This is the true joy of life, the being used for a purpose recognized by yourself as a mighty one; the being thoroughly worn out before you are thrown on the scrap heap; the being a force of Nature instead of a feverish selfish little clod of ailments and grievances complaining that the world will not devote itself to making you happy.

George Bernard Shaw, *Man and Superman*

HEATHER TOSTESON

INTRODUCTION: SURPRISED BY JOY

When we ran the call for this anthology, we posed it as both an invitation and a challenge. An invitation because joy is a deeply pleasurable state to experience and to recall, one that in times of contention and frustration and anxiety may feel inaccessible but also sorely needed. It is also a challenge to write about because one of the most striking things about positive emotions, of which joy is among the most powerful, is that they are in general non-verbal. When outraged or disappointed, we cry out, vent, erect towering arguments that we flail like blunt instruments, tell our own story incessantly. When we are very happy, we may leap with joy, yell with glee, we enact and vocalize, but we don't have a driving need to verbalize, rationalize, explain. Consequently, these positive emotions, so formative and necessary for fostering the deepest delights of life, often aren't explored as fully as they could be, their wisdom disregarded.

My own interest in joy may paradoxically come from my familiarity with depression. In his poem "Joy and Sorrow" Kahlil Gibran reminds us that these states are often twinned: "Together they come, and when one sits, alone with you at your board, remember that the other is asleep upon your bed." So often in my own life, particularly in those dark times, I would find myself— when all my intense will was exhausted, all my hopes in shreds, my good intentions erased—surprised by joy, by something rising inside me, quiet, clear, intrinsically positive, assured. I knew the indisputable reality of the pain I was in, and at the same time felt seamlessly healed. I wanted that warmth, that intrinsic certainty, with my whole being and knew it was not within my power to will or to create—but here it was, independent of anything I had done or could do, filling me with the deepest sense of well-being. At those moments, to paraphrase Robert Browning, I was sure that life meant and meant intensely and meant good and that I was an indisputable part of that meaning, that good, in ways I didn't understand fully but could not ignore or deny. From that insight, the quiet certainty of it, the calm delight of it, other insights followed, but that moment was enough. That state was enough. I didn't have to earn it—indeed I couldn't—and it wasn't conditional on my will, my behavior, my level of faith. What I did have some control over was how fully I would open to it, become one with it, allow myself to be changed by it.

Thinking about joy these last few months, I began to make a list of moments of deep joy in my life. What I found was that as I began to recall these moments, more followed. Psychologists call this mood-contingent memory retrieval. When we're sad our lives can feel like an unbroken train of failures, disappointments, misjudgments. When we're happy, we see a path of love given and received, challenges met. This dynamic was very clear to me one autumn in my forties. I was at a difficult period in my life. My son grown, I'd moved to a new city, new state, taken a job that was a bad fit. I had rented a weekend getaway in the Georgia mountains. Often, distraught at my situation, I would hike the mountain in the nearby state park. As I struggled up the steep slope, I would be frantically thinking about what I could do to fix things, and the more frantically I thought, the more clearly I could see my whole life stretching out behind me—an unbroken series of poor choices, bad luck, inadequacy, disappointment, and my future a natural continuation of the same. There would come a point, at the top of the slope, when I would pause, breathless, totally helpless. I would be staring out blankly into the trees, catching a glimpse of the next mountain, and the next, the next, and inexplicably something came to meet me. A whole new feeling set. I began to see another path through my life, one where I had a body that could climb a hill, I had will, agency, hope, a history of resilience, love. I would scramble back down the mountain making plans, seeing options, chugging away like the little engine that could.

What originally fascinated me about the nature of this shift was how complete it was—and how binary. And how reliable it was in its own way: enough exertion, enough endorphins, and the parasympathetic system kicks in, and with it a different world view. What interests me now is the exact moment of shift, that moment when I just stopped because I had no more drive, no solutions, no escape, that moment when I was just there, alone at the top of the mountain, breathing, receiving, aware of the light on a leaf, the song of a bird, a rustle in the underbrush, the sun slipping behind a cloud or emerging from it, how in some ways that moment is very similar to joy—and how it is not. What interests me now is the mystery of that pause, whether there is a third path we can chart through our lives that is made up of moments like that. How would that third path differ from the binary ones of sadness and happiness? What are the unique qualities of joy that would inform it?

❋   ❋   ❋

The first quality of joy is found in the title of this anthology. Surprise. We are always surprised by joy. It's not something we can will into existence. C. S. Lewis, making a distinction between joy and happiness, says "joy is never in our power, and pleasure often is." There is always an element of awe in joy—awe as wonder, not dread. An essential dimension of joy is that we find ourselves in relation to something greater and more profoundly positive than our conscious minds.

Another striking quality of joy is a feeling of completeness. There is an inner stillness in moments of joy, a listening inside and out that is trusting, appreciative. There is no yearning, no *saudade*, in joy. We have a sense of integrity, wholeness, repleteness. We know ourselves at that moment as enough and that awareness is wonderful, more than enough. There is an observation I encountered through the somatic movement and awareness technique of Feldenkrais that has kept coming back to me as I muse on the nature of joy: We can so organize in the pursuit of something we cannot receive it when it comes. But in the state of joy, we are organized to receive, and to receive what we may never have dared hope for: *Enough*

Another essential quality of joy is that it is meaningful. There is an intellectual dimension to joy that is tied up with the sense of wonder, an aha, just so, quality. We get something with our whole being—muscles and senses and mind; we experience a larger understanding of ourselves, our lives, our purpose, our right relation with existence. "This is the true joy of life, the being used for a purpose recognized by yourself as a mighty one," George Bernard Shaw reminds us. Joy turns our attention to the source of that larger purpose.

Joy is very private, but it attaches us. In some ways it is the opposite of ecstasy. We're not taken out of ourselves, we draw the world in and we let it draw us out too. Our awareness is kinesthetic and expansive. We're located in the moment, keenly aware, delighted. This isn't a crafted experience. We don't want to block anything out, escape anything, transcend. Wonder grounds us. It also makes us grateful.

As I made my list of the many moments in my life when I had been surprised by joy, I noticed another quality that feels especially important: timelessness. The insights that I had at those moments are still fresh, surprising, persistent. They have a call to them still. Usually when I remember my life (unless I'm in the grips of serious mood-contingent memory retrieval), my mind pulls up both positive and negative core events, and also what followed the happiness, what followed the sorrow, in other words it follows the natural oscillations of time. What followed qualifies my evaluation of the preceding state. But that is not true with these moments of joy. Something in them stays fresh, untouched—as surprising and as relevant as it was at the time.

For example, at the moment of my son's birth, I felt very detached as I saw him flail, slick and bloody and howling, in the doctor's hands. I had had a very rapid delivery preceded by two hours of intense oxygen-sapping transition that had been denied by everyone around me. A medical student had solemnly told me that I might have to endure this for twenty-four hours, a nurse had told me I imagined my waters had burst. No one was prepared, least of all me, when I announced I had to push. So from a great distance, I watched my son, heard him, and thought, I need to tell him, "It is not so bad to be alive." It truly was all the wisdom I, a shaken twenty-one year old, had to give.

But when my son was set beside me, when his skin touched mine, I felt us both washed by something luminous and still, and I felt something clear and absolute and yes, joy-filled, rise in me and I heard myself say, "I *want* you to be here." There has never been a moment in the forty-five years of his existence that those words, meant for me as well as for him, have ceased to resonate. When I remember that moment, I feel we were both being held, that what I said came through me, organized me anew, organized me to receive.

One reason that insights we derive from our moments of joy remain unqualified over time may be that they transcend our understandings of both joy and sorrow. This is not a sentimental state, rather a faithful one, described in one of Martin Buber's Hasidic tales this way: ". . . one who is truly joyful is like a man whose house has burned down, who feels his need deep in his soul and begins to build new. Over every stone that is laid, his heart rejoices."

Joy, although an expansive state, one that makes us feel deeply attached to the world, is also experienced as very individualized and private. We naturally respond that way when we see someone in a state of joy. Our instinct is not to approach too closely, it feels intrusive to do so. If we do approach, we do so carefully, quietly as if the calm of their inner delight has calmed us too. We may make eye contact, smile, touch someone briefly, lightly. We may look where they are looking, attuning to their wonder. In this sense, joy can be considered contagious.

Around my birthday last year, I found myself in a sustained period of psychological reorganization. I decided to acknowledge this by releasing a balloon a day for each year of my life, just to acknowledge how long it takes to release sustained habits, stances toward the world. Every day as I released a balloon, I would release something, a doubt, a regret, an intention, a thanks, an insight, a delight. Sixty-seven years is a long time to live I quickly understood, as did the patient women and men at the dollar stores who filled the batches of balloons I bought, week after week, after week. The real discipline here was that I had to watch each balloon until it disappeared completely from sight. Some seemed determined to snag themselves in the tall trees surrounding our house, others wafted back and forth over the roof for a long time, some surged off to the right, the left. No two ascents were alike. As I watched each unique trajectory something would shift in me, some space would open. It was the particularity and the unpredictability of each path that entranced me. When I think back fondly on this ritual now, I wonder if this might have been my way of cultivating my capacity for joy. And perhaps not mine alone.

To celebrate my birthday we went to the coast, so I released balloons over the ocean on a mysteriously calm, cloudless morning. (I was behind, so I had three to release.) Hands shading my eyes I stood in the shallows, watching each surprisingly slow ascent. It felt like there wasn't even a breath of wind, but each balloon chose a different route into the great blue. There wasn't a single cloud in the sky, nothing to distract me from the red, or blue, or gold globe turning, pausing, shifting right, shifting left. As I watched, there was an expanding awareness of the breadth of the horizon, the height of the arcing sky, the surprising warmth of the November sun, the invitation in the surreal stillness. When I finally turned around, I found that my husband and other people on the beach had begun to watch the balloons' slow, distinctive ascents with as much interest as I had. Time shifted. Something in our relationship with each other shifted. Without words. But if there were words, I think they would be a variant of the ones that flowed through me at my son's birth: I *want* to be here, exactly here, exactly as I am, now.

❄   ❄   ❄

Where do we find joy? More exactly, where does it find us? The various subjects that organize this anthology—children, identity, family, intimacy, the quotidian, community, illness, nature, illumination—give us some idea. Everywhere. And not when we're expecting it, pursuing it. But joy is such a gracious experience, so lasting in its effects, we can't help but wonder if there are ways to cultivate a sensitivity, an openness to it.

Clearly there are some states that are more conducive to joy: receptive or contemplative states when we are observing the world around us not as a means but as an end in itself. Whatever I may have chosen to add to my balloons in terms of intention, symbolism, over those sixty-seven days, it was the balloons themselves that became the source of fascination, the vagaries of the wind, the clouds, the hide and seek of the sun. Ends in themselves. When we are understanding ourselves in this way, as complete, *enough*, and are free to look out instead of in; when we see our families in this way, as sources of mystery and surprise; when we pause on a mountainside and look around at a beauty that we have had no hand in making but that speaks our deepest truths in a way that can't be gainsaid; when we hear and accept a dire prognosis and know in our diseased bones, our tired hearts, that life is not lost to us until we are lost to it—we are making a home for joy. These are practices associated with spirituality, mindfulness—and also creativity. I believe many artists experience the act of making in much the same way. "Not me, but the wind that blows through me," is how D. H. Lawrence describes it in his poem, "Song of a Man Who Came Through." Each of the artists writing here is asking us to share in their wonder at that wind, the gift of it.

❄   ❄   ❄

Why is it important to create an anthology around joy, to lift up such an intensely private, essentially unpredictable emotional state, however positive this calm delight, this delicious fruit of the spirit? Why is it important to lift it up together?

I would suggest it is because we suffer as a society from a limited vocabulary for the more profound positive emotions. We don't have the words to describe, refine, and appreciate them. We are all given extensive vocabularies with which to describe our wants and desires, but not our pleasures, our gratitudes, our haves. We need a vocabulary as granular and as powerful as the one we have for the challenges, trials, tribulations, disappointments and betrayals of our lives to describe the richness of our lives, the gifts, the wonders, the surprises, the sweet delights, the fullness, the worth.

The practices by which we make room for joy—the quieting, the looking around us, the listening, the receptivity, the focus on the world, including ourselves, as a mystery not a means—all invite us into a very different relationship with ourselves, our experience, and each other. What if instead of sharing our discontents, dreads, and despairs, bonding over what we're seeking, missing, have a right to, we began sharing the fruits of our experiences of joy with each other?

What would happen if we were to ask people we know to describe a moment in their life when they were surprised by joy and listened to them with the purpose of sharing their focus, sharing their wonder? What if we asked whether that experience of joy left behind some lasting traces, a belief or understanding that has influenced their choices, that has become a source of wisdom for them? What if we started to build together on these experiences of deep delight, calm, wantedness, experiences that didn't happen because we willed them, that can't be ascribed to our conscious, intentional selves?

What if we as a society were all to talk less about the righteous pursuit of happiness and the myriad threats to it we're constantly mobilizing against, and focus instead on the mystery of enough? Focus on the wind that blows through us? Not just as individuals, but as a society? Where have we as citizens each experienced an unsought, transforming moment of calm delight, integrity, coherence, right relation, *enough*? What if we, as a people, were to listen for, cultivate, and follow that third path through our shared life, one that includes humility, gratitude and wonder?

I. CHILDREN

JOAN DOBBIE

I THINK MY GRANDS ARE THE GREATEST
For Mara, Seth and Lyla

It's because of their love
& because of their laughter

I mean one of them falls
& the other one kisses

or one of them wins
& the other one dances
      & cheers & holds up two thumbs!

or one of them loses
& the other two huddle in close

(whispering love words
until she's stopped crying)

& after we've all watched the
Peanuts Movie for just about two hours straight

the three of them leap to their feet
& they dance & they dance

I mean real classy dancing
(I'm thinking Jackson Five, that really is
what I'm thinking)

& when mom says okay kids it's bedtime they
do crawl obediently into their sleeping bags

though not quite into their beds because
there at the top of the carpeted stairs

sits young Prince Temptation &
down
  down
    down
      they go sleeping bag sliding
bumpedy
  bumpedy
    bumpedy bump

all the way down to the living room floor
laughing like crazy

MARGARET HASSE

WATER SIGN

Two-year-old Charlie loves water,

loves the force of water
in gutters, pipes, the second hose
bought to keep peace between brothers
who spray tomatoes with the intensity
of fire fighters at a five alarm fire,

loves the sources of water:
faucet, penis, rain, spit.

He longs like a pilgrim for wet places
where his worship is
complete submersion:
bathtub, swim pool, lake.

To praise water,
he secludes himself in the bathroom.
Ascending a stepping stool to the sink,
he opens valves to an endless rush
of new pressure in copper pipes.

So *much* water, why not share it?
Give it away until it seeps
through the floorboards,
showers into the kitchen,
fills the bowls on the table,
flows on the heads
of his amazed mother and brother

who do not immediately recognize
that grace might descend like this—
inconveniently–
from a complete enthusiast
who needs to be forgiven
for being generous
with whatever he loves.

CLAUDIA VAN GERVEN

BABY AT THE WINDOW

How glorious, the way the sun guilds his face
How his face crimsons the sun. There are no

words for this—literally *no* words—just an
encounter between light and enlightenment

There's a quiet recognition in this gaze over
Everything he doesn't know, a greeting of one

Immense soundless regard spilling into another
The earth will bend the sky another way and

the boy will lose his sweet sunshiney cheeks
The chubby fingers that rest on the sill will

learn to throw a ball and tease the cat, but
for now only this one solitary boy in this one

unrepeatable window becoming at one with
this single, silent, momentous, meaningless

     forever

LAUREN K CARLSON

ON MOTHER'S DAY

my son tries to break an egg
he grips it in his fist
as though he could squeeze it open

but finding the egg
resistant to even-sided pressures

he strikes
the roundest end against
the counter's edge
with force

the resulting cracks
grant his small hand
a crushing power

membranes burst
past shattered shell-white
yolk bleeds down
his arm

his face grows like a plant
toward light

"See?"

As if he broke sunshine
over every valley on earth

As if he brought morning
to his mother in a silver bowl

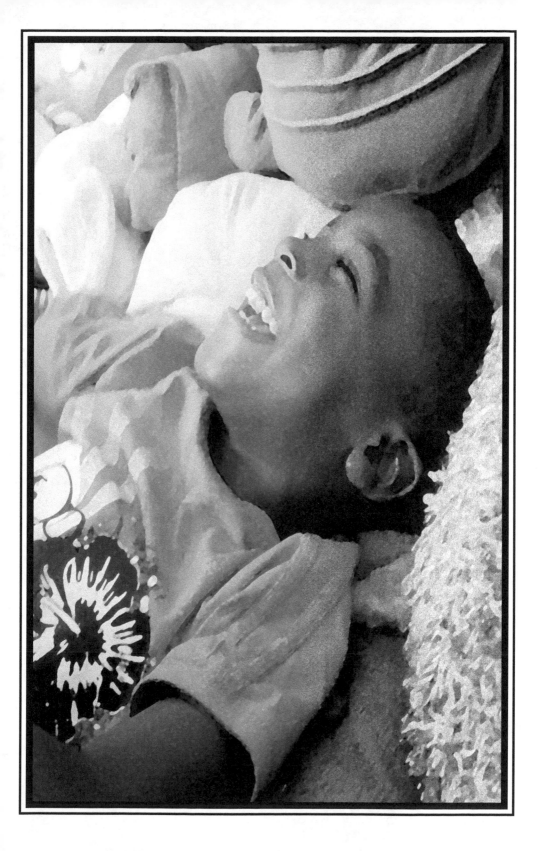

PEGI DEITZ SHEA

BOY MAKES IMPRESSION:

(Upon viewing *Luxe, Calm et Volupté* by
Henri Matisse, at Musée D'Orsay, Paris)

Little boy, hand yanked
by father, yawns,
drags his feet in a portrait gallery.
But once he's through
a portal, his eyes
the size of oysters:
"Papa, les Pointillists!"

He runs close
enough to kiss
one of six female nudes
dining seaside
with a fully clothed man.
The museum guard,
a woman, does not move.

The boy backpedals
across the room.
Grande dames, students,
lovers grant him space.
He opens his arms
to frame the painting.
Then he dashes
close enough to sniff
a bare foot toeing the sand.
The guard does not move.

The child repeats his study:
His fingers comb the bather's hair,
he nibbles the fruits and cheeses,
his arms embrace the work.

Finally he stops and,
taking his father's hand,
declares, "Papa, each nipple
has only one point."
The museum guard says,
"Touché."

LOWELL JAEGER

WONDROUS WORLD

Many wonders I've beheld in this wondrous world
of canyons and chasms and summits of sculpted snow.
None so radiant, so indelible, as my daughter,
nine years old, perched on a granite ledge, dangling her legs,
awash in sunshine above a slope of scree slanting
into an alpine meadow of riotous and frantic blooms.

I'd left her there while I scouted our most favorable
path of descent. And navigated to her side again
by the music of her song—a child's song she'd learned
for the pageant at school. Her bird-like voice in the breeze
amidst the incense of nectar. Her smile and rejoicing
wave upon my return. A dozen mountain goats,

curious, nosing closer, transfixed to witness
this ever-unfolding wondrous world. Where I,
like the goats, paused in reverence. And like the goats,
I inched forward toward her, while clouds above
continued to flow, and blossoms widened
to the sky's melodious allure. And beneath us

ancient strata rose toward daylight through dark.

GENESIS

In the beginning, at the kitchen table,
my three children with paper and crayons,
shoulders bent low and hands fisting
the task before them.

Lo, through the wide windows
the morning shown down upon artistic intentions,
and the sun's slant rays rained
a glittered drift of pine pollen, spray of stardust,
as pages transformed, filled

with trees of leafy green, turquoise lake and sky, purple-grey
cluster of clouds enshrouding the highest reaches
of a distant craggy range. Whole neighborhoods
begotten. Barns. Fenced acres of spotted cattle, grazing.

And birds everywhere. I could hear them sing
as I passed through the room on this day
of creation, pulled on my boots, opened the door,
to behold the vastness, the particulars, the swirl

and churn of genesis, circumstance and inspiration,
my children and their children and theirs awash
in the world's possible outcomes, joyously enraptured, laboring
to guide the butterfly—this one colored orange/yellow —

supping from a tall flower,
which hath blossomed bold and blood red.
That one. Corner of the garden.
Edge of the page. Right there.

II. IDENTITY

HEATHER TOSTESON

WE'RE ALL DONORS HERE

"You are essential to our success," they told us in the training course. "We're a non-profit, sure, but we need to break even. We provide a service that is half animal science, half romance. The romance is the clincher for everyone concerned. We need these guys to keep coming back—and much as they think it's for the cash, and tell anyone who asks the same, they're bound to experience some push back, some remorse. It's your job to make them seem attractive, genuine, a little noble."

Noble for jerking off twice a week to a porn video or a porn magazine in an empty room? I think.

"For jerking off all by their lonesome for a full year. Don't think it doesn't get to them. They feel virile at first. After awhile they can feel perverted, exploited. Your job is to write them up so they, and our clients, see them as loveable, *dateable*."

"Three-quarters of our clients are lesbians," a woman in army fatigues and a buzz cut, whose first name is Lacey but who prefers to be known as Wilson, protested.

"They're pretty adept by now at making gender translations," Delores said. She's our trainer. Delores is gorgeous. Long curly black hair down to mid-back, brown skin, tight jeans and a tight sequined T-shirt. She's a performance poet in her real life—but her poems are all stories, she emphasizes. She has an MFA from San Francisco State. She's here because her boyfriend has a three-year post-doc at Emory. He's in neuroscience and is going to be their financial bulwark and ballast, she says.

"And they're susceptible. You'd be surprised. We were. Our sales went up dramatically when we began including the interviews. The donors' own narratives weren't half as effective. The guys came out, well, like you might expect. Like guys. Self-absorbed and a little boastful, or terse and flat. But when *we* described their physical appearance (muscular or tall, thin or broad shouldered, dimples, long lashes, a little tattoo showing under a neat blue shirt, a swagger or contagious laugh) or their attitude (withdrawn but slowly warming up, especially when talking about a beloved mother, grandmother, or younger sister; or brash but also self-aware with a keen sense of humor) something changed all around. The orders came rushing in. The guys completed their contracts and brought in referrals.

"And we, my dears, all of us starving writers, became indispensable," Delores said with a broad inclusive gesture to the four of us, which set her sixteen glittering bangles ringing. "But this is the course they don't give you in college or grad school, the one that puts a transforming gloss on real life. I need to tell you before we begin, it's contagious. It begins to infiltrate your whole life and, I'm sorry to say, your writing. Bid adieu to MFA angst and arid superiority—as if the meaninglessness of the universe is your own private secret. Think *juicy*. Two adjectives where once you used none. Think cute, adorable, charming, magnetic. Think women's romance fiction. Think prepubescent girls gushing over Justin Bieber."

We began to look at our hands, the door.

Delores, who knew her audience, looked at us with a gentle smile. "It's not *that* bad."

It was primarily a writing class. We were paired off in twos and asked to write a description of each other, from wide forehead and widow's peak to heart-shaped mouth and sensuous lips, arched or straight brows, strong or pointed chins. Hair texture, not just color. Touchable was a texture. Clothes, hipster or Green Peace, Occupy Wall Street or Goizueta Business School wasn't enough. Black pants, tight, with a beige metrosexual cardigan or green zippered hiker's pants and a plaid shirt.

We also had an interviewing class. We were taught how to create a comfortable interview environment, even in a fairly sterile office. A plant on a window sill—lucky bamboo or a flower without much scent, like carnations or daisies. Kleenex. A water heater, tea, real cups. Cookies on a plate. A warm but neutral expression.

We were told to tell them right off that our job was to get to know them so we could write a warm and positive description of them that would help interested clients know why *we* thought they would be a good choice for progenitor of that client's son or daughter.

"Be careful not to use the word father," Delores said, "except with the ones who are willing to be identified. Even then, it is best to use the word donor. Emphasize the other family relationships. Do they have a favorite brother or sister? What do they like about the relationship?"

She sat down in front of us and pulled her chair up. She had added a black sweater, still low cut. She leaned over so we could see the effects of her push-up bra. "The real secret here is that you have to let yourself be, for that hour, the person, the sensibility that *needs* them, their particular gifts, *their* quirks. So, honestly, we're looking for people as whole-hearted and promiscuous with their affections as labradors. In other words, fiction writers or playwrights. No poets. Or memoirists. They're inveterate solipsists."

"This isn't about you," Delores scolded us more than once. "You are just a conduit, a match maker. But to do this, you have to be in touch with what is most seductive and susceptible in yourself."

We left the two-day course as jazzed and confident as we were supposed to leave our interviewees.

"I can't believe your good luck, *mijita*," my mother told me. "So many young people these days, even with these college degrees, there is no employment. And here are you, your first week out of school, already helping to pay the rent. Using your *mind*, not your hands."

My mother is a maid, has been as long as I can remember, but her hours at the Hilton have been cut with the recession. My dad recently returned to Chiapas because he was worried about the new law they've passed here. I was born here, so I can still go to school but my two older brothers are undocumented and have left Georgia with their families. So I'm all Mamí has now.

We've rented out two of the rooms in the house, but the five guys who are staying here don't feel like family. It's like *we're* the renters. We come in at night and they're all sitting in the living room watching TV, filling the chairs where my dad and brothers used to sit. My nieces and nephews aren't around. It's just Univision, Telefutura, and occasional laughter. Everybody's in bed by nine, except on weekends, and out of the house by six. They're an intrusion, but they're also seasonal workers, and when they leave, I'm not sure how we'll make it. I almost told Mamí that I'm paid on an emission basis, but that made me feel creepy. If I were it would be about 20% of what each of the guys I am interviewing gets for "active" ejaculate. I wish they had told me that when I took my GREs.

I think about these guys in our living room quietly watching a telenovela and consider suggesting that they participate. I could get a referral fee. I could do the interviews. You're supposed to be in college or technical school, but I could fake that for them, claim they all received degrees back home. It's not like they make people bring in their diplomas. But you have to be able to work legally in the state, and I'm not sure any of them qualify. They're braver than my brothers, or more desperate. And not as tied down. Both my brothers have legal wives and kids. So they stand to lose everything if they're deported. By the time they get back in, their kids will have forgotten them. That matters to us. Families stay together. It hurts my mom to think of my dad all alone in Mexico. As soon as I can stand on my own two feet, for example, my mom is going to join him. That's a joke. You'd get it immediately if you saw me.

I know they're experimenting now with injecting stem cells in your spinal column, but I am in a wheelchair for life. When I was fourteen, my dad and I were driving to Walmart and there was an accident. It wasn't anyone's fault. A car had a blowout and the driver lost control and steered into our truck and then we rammed into a semi in the next lane. My dad will never forgive himself. He feels he should have swerved the other way—but if you just try and imagine it, I mean in reality, the physics of the whole thing, there wasn't anything he could have done. It's just that he came out in one functioning piece and his beloved daughter did not. It broke his heart and even I can't mend it for him. It's one of the times when the fatalistic reflexive makes sense: *Mi espina se rompió. El corazón de mi papa se quebró.* My spine broke itself. My dad's heart shattered itself.

It was as good an injury as you could hope for, I suppose. The break is pretty low, T-11, and incomplete. So I can feel below that even though I can't walk. My pelvis wasn't shattered like Frida Kahlo's (although she was able to walk). I don't get to wear those fancy plaster casts she decorated so dramatically or to keep a mirror over my bed.

It's odd, since I'm the one who got hurt, but it's clear to all of us that it is my job to make this better, bearable, for everyone. I've taken my role seriously, and it's helped me. It means that I'm the only member of my family to finish high school, let alone college—or a masters. They are *all* so proud of me. My brothers came back for my last graduation ceremony. They left their wives and kids in Illinois, but they were here, cheering. My dad left for Chiapas the day after. I offered him my diploma, but he said he wanted me to keep it here. It was safer. None of them know they supported me in getting what must be one of the most worthless degrees on earth. So it's my job to make sure that the cost isn't too high, that my mother gets reunited with my dad as soon as possible. They're good with each other, my parents. It's what I'd call a murmuring love. Not lots of *mi amor, mi reina* or *mi cielo*. Just this constant undercurrent, as much tone as actual words, *"¿Tortillas?" "Sí."* *"¿Huevos?" "Gracias." "Aquí es la renta."*

When I wrote stories in grad school, I wrote about all of them. What it was like for my dad at twenty to leave his village in Chiapas for the first time. What it was like for my mom to follow him eight years later—bringing my brothers, they were seven and nine, in through the desert. How my brothers met their wives. I could see everyone in the class was waiting for me to describe why I was in a wheelchair, but I never did. It just isn't that interesting to me. I'd rather write about them, their prurient curiosity, what they imagine might have happened. I've introduced myself into this story more than in any other I've written. It's my try at experimental fiction (which mainly means lost in the *ombligo*) and is quickly boring me. I want more options than this one body, this one life offer me. I think I wanted this as intensely at twelve as I do now, so in the most profound way my character hasn't changed because of the accident, if anything it has become more itself.

My thesis advisor, Antonio Rosario, was also Hispanic, but third generation, all of them educated, which he complained was not so good for his writing. "Now you," he said, "have primary source material." He kept fondling my stories in a way that made me feel he was touching something else.

He told me that if I sequenced my stories right, added one or two more, I'd have a novel-in-stories, which would be more marketable than short stories. "Once you have 200 or 250 solid pages, just send it out. Contests. Publishers. Agents. Be promiscuous, polymorphous perverse. The worst that can happen is that it will be rejected. Don't do it, though, until you're two-thirds of the way through your next book," he warned me.

His first book had been published to quite a bit of small press hoopla about eight years ago. He was too busy to write another, he said. He regularly applied for one hundred writing jobs a year. His wife Karen worked as a librarian at Georgia State. He was the primary care-giver for their two-year-old daughter. Karen, beautiful, blonde, with a little of the reserve of Catherine Deneuve, was jealous of me. I could feel it when I ran into them on campus together. But I'm not sure whether it was because of my relationship with Antonio or with their daughter, Cielo, who loved to climb up on my wheelchair and take a ride with me—and had learned to smother me with kisses as petition, bribe, and payment all rolled into one. Cielo was adopted. From Guatemala. She looked a little like me. My family is Mayan, like her.

Karen was the one who couldn't conceive. Antonio told me they had gone through her whole trust fund trying to find out what was wrong. They were thinking of an egg donor so she could have the experience of pregnancy. He looked at me a long time after he said that. I was glad Karen wasn't there. There are romantics who gloss reality like Delores said, and there are romantics who deny it entirely. I could see clearly into which category Antonio fell—and I wanted to be in another. When I graduated, I lied and told him I was returning to Mexico with my parents, that I'd be gone at least a year. Atlanta is a big, sprawling city. As long as I avoid the campus, it could be years, perhaps decades before our paths cross again.

I suppose that experience *is* what made me apply for the job at the sperm bank. That unvoiced suggestion about being an egg donor. What use, Antonio implied by his silence, were those eggs to me? He has no idea. The doctors have said that there is no reason why I can't, with adequate medical supervision, conceive and carry a baby to term—or care for it. This has always been a most secret source of hope for me. It is, along with consoling my family, why I have studied so long and so hard.

I think there was something about Antonio's silence, the rapaciousness of it, that was as decisive to me as the moment in the hospital when the doctor told me that I would not be able to walk again. I mean, I *knew* I wasn't going to be able to walk, but there was something in the saying of it, in all that would be set in motion once it was out in the air like that, that created a brave new world for me. One that brought out the best in me. One that let me claim my strength. Antonio's implying that my whole life was destined to be one of all give and no take, the write-off in it, did something similar. What had been a secret source of hope for me was now going to be an open one.

When I interview those young men, I *am* going to be one of those potential mothers. More than that, I am going to have those mothers see the world through *my* eyes for a moment. I am going to write about how these young men walk, when they pause to reflect, when they make eye contact, when they stare at the door, what they probably looked like as babies, as boys of three or nine or thirteen. And these young men, having lost themselves in my attention like Narcissus in a pond, will when they read what I've written be surprised into an image of themselves that is a little tougher, more sharply focused, more robust.

I can't wait to start. I decide I'm going to practice on our boarders and roll my wheelchair into the living room, station it in front of the television. "*Caballeros,*" I begin, "*necesito su ayuda.*" I gesture for them to turn off the television. "If we are to make the rent this month, I need to practice my interview skills," I tell them.

I explain the sperm bank to them. They are stunned. Only in America. But they want me, like a sister, a daughter, to succeed. They don't know I have an ulterior motive. I am harvesting their stories as Antonio wanted to harvest me. But unlike him, I want to give them something in return.

"I need to have you tell me why you think any woman should choose you to father her child." The bright bangles on my wrist clatter as I arrange my long red skirt. My earrings glitter. My long black hair flows like water over my full breasts. I have their full attention. I have degrees. Citizenship. English. And the power to raise others up like me.

"Roberto?" I ask. He is the oldest, the leader. He is in his late forties, but looks ten years older. He comes from Guerrero. He has six children. His oldest son, Dionisio, is with him this trip. Roberto is a gentle man, his hands worn from work in the peach orchards and tomato fields. He is missing the first joint on his right ring finger. He has built a house of cement with his own hands. He can't read but he can recite all the psalms from memory, and many Juan Gabriel songs as well. When he smiles, it's as if the light is falling in saints' rays through dark clouds.

"*Soy honesto,*" he tells me. "*Leal, cariñoso.*"

His son Dionisio nods. "*Humilde,*" he adds.

"And determined and intelligent," I add. Roberto smiles, blushes.

When he starts telling me about his childhood, the dirt floor, the smell of pine smoke from the fire, the sweetness of his mother's tamales, a silence circles us. I can hear my pen moving over the paper.

"And as a father, what is your *don*, Don Roberto?" I ask.

Dionisio laughs. "He loves and leaves. Loves and leaves. Nobody ever gets tired of him."

And sends money home, Roberto adds. Every week. *Por la leche y el techo.*

My mother comes in, settles herself in a chair at the table. There is a gentle glow from the summer twilight lighting us both, a dignity to our separateness. She can see, finally, that it is safe to leave, that I too, have a *don*, a gift, that can't be taken from me, that replenishes itself through its giving, like a fountain, and that is as visible to others as it is to her, as it will be to my own daughter. I have *room* for the world—and the world has room for me.

TERRY SANVILLE

A NEW BEGINNING

Sometime way past midnight, they packed us into trucks, maybe six or seven rumbling deuce-and-a-halfs, and headed for the airport at Biên Hòa. Nobody talked. Nobody wanted to jinx our departure. 365 days was definitely enough. We roared along deserted roads and passed through a Vietnamese village, shacks built of scrap corrugated metal and packing crates. As we drove by one shack, I caught flashes from a color television and wondered if our western trinkets would be the only things left behind when the war finally ended.

The trucks rolled through a series of gates and onto a concrete apron where a commercial jetliner rested with stairs attached to its front and rear. We jumped down onto the pavement and formed two lines. I was the last soldier in the one that led to the plane's rear entrance. We inched forward, with the scrape of our boots and low mutterings the only sounds.

Finally, I climbed the stairs. At the top I stepped onto the plane and turned left. The jet's cabin extended in a one-point perspective into the distance. The soldiers in front of me quickly grabbed seats . . . the last seats. I stared down the aisle and couldn't see any gaps in the sea of closely cropped heads. A chill shook me. Would I have to wait for another plane, spend another minute, hour, day in that terrible place? I told myself that I'd fly the whole damn way home in the latrine, in the coat closet, in the plane's wheel well strapped to the landing gear. It didn't matter. But I would not spend a second longer in Vietnam.

From the far end of the cabin a stewardess waved her hands over her head. I pushed toward her and she pointed to a seat near the front. I plopped down and attached the lap belt, pulled it snug, and sucked in deep breaths. I folded my arms so that the guys around me couldn't see how badly my hands shook.

We waited . . . and waited some more. Finally, the ground crew removed the stairs, the doors closed, and the plane began to roll. It stopped and turned at the end of the runway. I tried breathing slow and steady. Then the surge of power, the roar from the engines, the thump thump thump of the wheels rolling faster and faster, then the liftoff and the clunk of the landing gear being retracted.

When that clunk sounded, the soldiers erupted into cheers and shouts of joy. It sounded more jubilant than any New Year's Eve celebration I'd ever experienced, which wasn't many since I'd just turned twenty-one, six months before.

The flight from Vietnam to Oakland, California took forever, flying north then east into the black sky. After two stops and more than eighteen hours, I deplaned in a stupor. The bitter San Francisco Bay winds chilled me. But after a year living in the super-humid tropics, the cold felt wonderful.

Most of us soldiers had dressed in light jungle fatigues and boots. But the military wouldn't release us into the civilian population wearing combat gear. We waited in a drafty building while Army tailors assembled dress green uniforms for each of us, complete with new black "low quarter" shoes and all the appropriate medals, ribbons, and patches affixed to our jackets.

Hours later they finally let me go. Myself and two other GIs grabbed a taxi and headed for San Francisco International Airport on the other side of the Bay. One of the guys wanted to catch a plane east to Kansas City. I felt lucky that Santa Barbara was only an hour-and-a-half flight south. But could I find a local flight? Or would I have to spend a night in the City at some fleabag hotel, waiting yet another day? And the closer I got to my home, the slower things seemed to move, and even minor delays felt excruciating.

But I lucked out. A coastal flight would leave in less than two hours. With my name placed on the standby list, I took a seat. Later, I was confirmed for boarding. I phoned home and let my parents know when I would arrive. As I sat in the airport terminal, passing strangers stared at me. Some smiled and nodded. Others that looked my own age glared and flashed the peace symbol. But no one spoke to me, except the airline staff. At the gate, a young woman who took my ticket said, "Welcome home, Specialist." I guess my new uniform, medals and dazed demeanor signaled to her that I'd been one of the lucky ones. I nodded and hustled down the ramp to board the plane and begin the first stage of my return to normalcy.

The plane jerked and swayed in strong crosswinds. The stewardess barely had time to serve a single round of drinks before we started our descent to the Santa Barbara airport. The turbo-prop banked hard, landed with a bump, and rolled to a stop just beyond the low wall that separated the Spanish-style terminal from the apron. The ground crew attached stairs and we filed off the plane and across the smooth concrete. I think I was the only soldier on that puddle-jumper.

Ahead, I spotted my parents waiting for me. My throat closed up and I got that pain in my chest that I'd sometimes get when strong emotions hit—feels almost like eating ice cream too fast. My father, a Marine sergeant during World War II and Korea, extended a hand and we shook, then we hugged, all three of us. Tears streaked my mother's cheeks. We didn't say much. Just being there was joyful enough. But I realized that, for the past year, my life had been put on hold, with no reason to plan a future until I came home. And now that day stretched out before me, to begin again. All over again.

LINDA HANSELL

LIGHTER THAN AIR

Tucked among the tall pine trees that hug Woods Pond in Maine lies a place where I was transformed by music and movement. A place where I spun a new version of myself, unleashing unexpected joy in the process.

It was the summer after my sophomore year of college, and I was spending a week as a scholarship student at Maine Folk Dance Camp, a week-long camp for people to learn and be immersed in international folk dancing. The camp's rustic timber-framed cabins and large main lodge were dotted throughout the woods on the forested property, with the scent of pine and spruce trees in the air. Sunlight filtered through the branches onto the pine needles covering the forest floor.

People of all ages (mostly older adults) came for a week to learn folk dances from around the world. The week I attended featured dances from Bulgaria and Switzerland, as well as waltzes, polkas, and other traditional folk dances. Each day, workshops were held in which dances were taught by expert teachers, and each night there was a dance party.

As a scholarship student at the camp, I worked in the kitchen and dining hall—setting tables, washing dishes, and cleaning up the dining area and kitchen. After my shifts of scrubbing and dishwashing, I was free to attend the workshops and evening dances.

I arrived at the camp feeling anxious and self-conscious, but also eager to immerse myself in the dancing. In college, I had become acutely aware of my tendency to hold back, to be reserved and apprehensive when I was in new situations and with new people. I worried about what people would think of me. I was bumping up against the protective shell I had built to shield myself from a childhood filled with critical comments about my appearance, mostly from my mother. To boost my self-confidence, I had started writing notes to myself in my journal, telling myself to not worry so much, to enjoy new experiences, to let things unfold naturally.

My dance camp experience did not get off to an auspicious start. When I stepped off the bus that delivered me to the camp entrance, no one greeted me. As I wandered among the pine trees with my suitcase looking for my cabin, I felt a familiar nervous clenching in my stomach and wondered if I had made a mistake. I hoped that I could follow my own advice and come out of my shell, let myself be seen, and enjoy the week. My first-day apprehensions increased when, upon entering my shared cabin, I walked in on a couple making love—illicitly, it appeared.

"Oh excuse me," I mumbled, mortified. I dropped my suitcase and quickly left the cabin, feeling very alone.

Reporting to the kitchen in the main lodge for my first work shift, I met the kitchen staff and was oriented to my tasks. The biggest part of my job was washing the large, greasy pots and pans after meals in the dining-hall kitchen. I was surprised by the weight of the industrial-sized cooking vessels. Cleaning and lifting the pots and pans out of the camp's deep kitchen sink proved to be a physical challenge. After a few meals, I got used to handling the giant metal hanging sprayer to soak the oatmeal and lasagna-encrusted commercial pots and pans before scrubbing them.

By the middle of the week, the campers had befriended me, and the head cook and kitchen staff appreciated my hard work. My initial feelings of isolation and fear began to abate. After each meal, upon completing my kitchen duties, I hung up my apron and joined the workshops and evening dances in the dance-hall cabin up the hill.

"You're a delightful young lady," one dancer told me.

"And very versatile," added another, referencing my dishwashing and dancing.

One evening at the dance party I had the good fortune to be asked to do a waltz with a tall, good-looking, and accomplished dancer from Ontario named Mark. He had a full head of brown hair with bangs that swept across his forehead, lapping his warm brown eyes. As we waltzed, Mark guided me around the dance floor effortlessly and gracefully, and I had the sensation I was flying. I could not feel my feet touching the floor. Our movements were perfectly in sync with one another, as if we were one body, not two.

We glided around the room in a blur of elegant motion, spinning like whirling dervishes. I vaguely saw the knotted-pine walls of the dance hall rush by out of the corner of my eye, but I kept my eyes locked on Mark's, both to keep from getting dizzy and to fully absorb his handsome features. I could see from Mark's smile and twinkling eyes that he was enjoying the dance, too. I absorbed the admiring gazes and smiles of the other dancers as they watched us. As we floated around the room, a double helix of confidence and joy spiraled up from my feet through my legs, suffusing my whole body. *This is sublime,* I remember thinking. *This is heaven. I now know what bliss feels like.*

Dancing with such a nimble and fluid partner, I became aware of my own skill as a dancer and a partner. I was surprised by the grace of my own body, an unexpected gateway to joy. Anne Morrow Lindbergh wrote in *Gifts from the Sea,* "One cannot dance well unless one is completely in time with the music, not leaning back to the last step or pressing forward to the next one, but poised directly on the present step as it comes." When I let myself release fully into the music and movement, I was not worrying about the future, what anyone thought of me, or the even the next step. My body knew what to do. I felt like the belle of the ball.

I have danced many waltzes since that long-ago summer, and some have come close to that moment of feeling suspended, of being lighter than air, but none have matched it for the unexpected suffusion of joy that made every atom of my body sing. It was worth washing every one of those dirty, weighty pots to experience that lightness, presence, and bliss. As I move forward in life, I try to remember that in life—as with dance—balance, ease, and joy come with letting the moment guide me, and not looking too far backward or forward.

DANIEL M. JAFFE

THE KISS

As I pull my shoulder away from his, it's the eyes that first reveal what he thinks, their downward glance at his black boots or mine, the disappointment in his eyes, then the sudden nervous rub of thumb against forefinger, the shift from foot to foot as if he wants to flee now that someone has—that I have—rejected his kiss because I know, because he's told me. He thinks this, and yes, I have rejected his kiss, but only because I am shy and this is a public place, a Washington D.C. hotel lobby with gray vinyl indoor-outdoor chairs on beige indoor-outdoor carpeting, plastic potted palms in the corners and busloads of Southern Baptists arriving for some convocation, to replace us, a group of gay writers who've just ended a conference of our own. Maybe the chairs and carpeting and palms and Baptists all in the nation's capital are precisely why I should have kissed him here in this hotel lobby, but being forty and residually afraid of scandal and bashing, I turned my cheek.

He's from San Francisco where gay men are not shy or fearful of scandal or bashing, or if they are afraid, they've learned to hide their fears the way others, men like me from Boston, have learned to hide parts of self. (Oh, I tell myself all the time, I've been out for years, participating in this non-discrimination campaign—employment, housing, adoption—and that, publishing articles in gay magazines under my own name, attending Boston's Gay Pride Parade each and every year for twenty years, watching from the sidewalk.) In San Francisco men wear their status—positive or negative—like Boy Scout merit badges of one kind or another; in Boston we keep merit badges at home for only old friends, not mere conference acquaintances, to see.

And I didn't wish to diminish his story of struggle—ten years, no symptoms but one cocktail no longer working, a new one to try when he gets home. I didn't want him to feel I was trying to trump him with my own story of modestly greater suffering—thirteen years, blindness in left eye, one bout of emaciation several years ago, a new cocktail that returned me to normal weight, the cocktail turning ineffective, another cocktail, now a third. I know the importance of feeling special in one's pain. Bostonians know. San Francisco communal pain versus Boston private pain. The continental divide.

I know he doesn't understand all this, thinks I don't kiss him on the mouth because I fear catching although one cannot catch from a kiss. He wants to declare this saliva fact, spit this saliva fact into my face, but he does not, I know, because this is a hotel lobby full of Southern Baptists in Washington D.C. and even though he'd love to show them how we men kiss, he'd hate to show them a bitchy queen in high gear.

It was just a good-bye kiss, two acquaintances from lectures on the miserable trend of gay publishing and workshops on how to change that trend, both men away from lovers left at home, neither man intending to fool around on the side but still lonesome in a strange city. Dinner together at a Thai restaurant the night before, a couple of beers in a crowded gay bar, a quick and clumsy hug at the hotel lobby elevators before saying goodnight (each maybe wondering: is this a pass or politeness? and which would I rather it be?). Scrambled eggs in the hotel coffee shop this morning, check-out one after the other at the registration desk and thanks for keeping me company and if you're ever in Boston, if you're ever in San Francisco, exchange of e-mail addresses scribbled on backs of conference name tags, and then he leans in for that goodbye kiss on the lips, not lustful or romantic but friendly, a wet San Francisco meaningless we're-both-gay-so-this-is-what-we-do goodbye peck, but I angle my head just enough to the side so that lips plant on cheek.

The quarantine-isolation look in his eyes as they glance downward at his black boots or mine, that look I wore years ago when the emaciation hit, when at friends' homes I was suddenly offered drinks in disposable paper cups.

I'll e-mail him tomorrow and tell him how much I hope to meet his lover one day, to introduce him to mine, but I know that after this near-miss kiss he will never reply. So despite the Southern Baptists milling by the busload around us in this Washington D.C. hotel lobby full of gray chairs, beige carpeting and plastic palms, I grab his cheeks in both hands, plant one smack on the lips and even slip in my tongue. A moment of frozen immobility, then his tongue moves in response, we embrace and kiss deeply in the lobby amidst what I imagine to be gaping Southern Baptists, but I can't tell because my eyes, both good eye and bad, are closed and I'm lost in this kiss that has become more than it was ever meant, by either of us, to be.

Tasting the ketchup he'd dribbled on his eggs, sucking in his tongue as proof that he was mistaken a moment ago, I know he's now thinking I deflected that first kiss in order to control a secret lust, that now control has been lost. This, too, is misunderstanding, but one we can accept, across the country in beds beside our respective lovers, whom we'll tell of this public hotel lobby kiss, he and I, each of us feeling modestly guilty, and alive.

MARK TARALLO

THOUGHTS AT NIGHTSHORE

Why does this horizon
jeweled with fishing boats,

and this array of visible stars
in stringy wisps of galaxies,

Make me happy, so happy,
to be alone?

Over my right shoulder,
a lopsided grin of a moon

whispers:
Shouldn't marry.

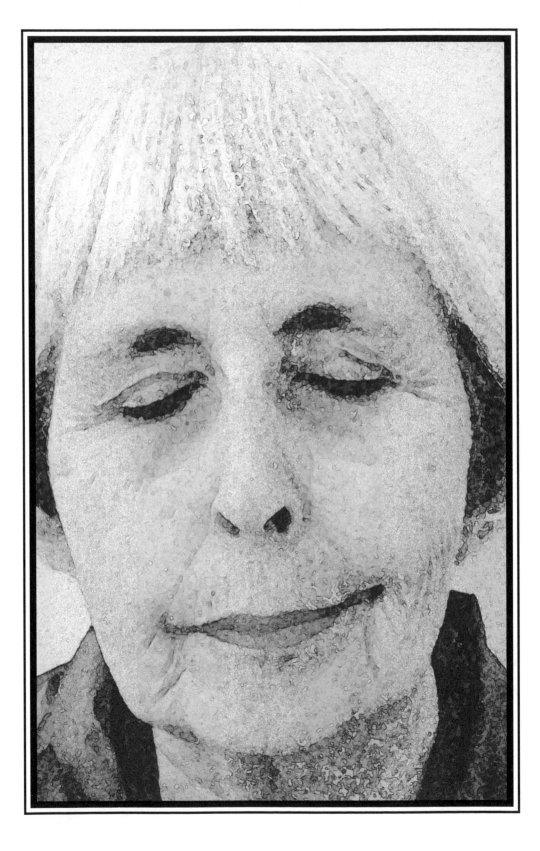

KERRY LANGAN

MY NAME IS YOUR NAME

She thinks of that article her son brought her to read. It said that if you can't remember something, think of things you associate with it. For instance, if you can't remember the name of an actress, think about what movies she was in and who her co-stars were. Our memories live in neighborhoods, the article concluded. "Oh, I don't give a hoot about some actress!" she'd said, tossing the magazine on her bed. She wonders if her son remembers the neighborhood where he grew up, all those years ago when her husband was still alive. When she closes her eyes, she can sometimes see it. There were shrubs in front of the porch, she's almost certain. Shrubs that grew so high that they blocked the house. A boy in the neighborhood climbed up one of the shrubs all the way up to the sky where he encountered a giant. She shakes her head. No, that's just a fairytale. That's not real.

Her name is Eleanor. Or Elizabeth. Think! she orders herself, but she still can't determine if she's Eleanor or her sister is. Her sister. She should call her sister. But, no, her sister died. A few years ago. No more than ten. Does it say Eleanor or Elizabeth on her gravestone? She needs to check the name engraved on it and then she will know what her own name is. She could ask her son what her first name is but he is so exasperated whenever she asks him a question. Or his eyes start to mist the way they did when he was a child and struggled with his reading. She'd made little signs and hung them all over their home, word labels for bed, table, chair, window, room, on and on. She'd sat with him for hours and hours, making up little stories about words so he could remember them. When he arrived home from school each day, she'd say, "Yellow, Charles" instead of "Hello, Charles." And he learned to respond, "Y-E-L-L-O-W, Mommy." She'd been relieved when math came easily to him.

Now she doesn't live in a neighborhood. She lives in a big house with too many people. Or she did until she left. The last thing she remembers about that place was that she was outside with some of the other people who lived there, all of them painting on big white poster boards propped on easels. She'd waited until the teacher, a young woman who smelled like orange peels, stopped beside her and said, "Oh, how nice." The picture was of a little blue house in a garden with pink flowers, the sun overhead partly hidden behind a fluffy cloud outlined in turquoise. "You have such a sense of color," the teacher told her. "Do you like pastels?" She'd answered, "I like all the colors." Heavens, she thought, the world would be such a dreary place if it were only black and white. Nodding, the teacher said, "You're absolutely right. All colors are beautiful," and moved on to the person next to her. She wished her son had heard the teacher say that: *You're absolutely right.* Then maybe he'd stop worrying about her. She'd wanted to sign the painting but she didn't know if she was Eleanor or Elizabeth. She lifted her brush and painted a blue "E" in the lower right corner. Then she set her brush down and got up. Looking over her shoulder, the teacher said, "We're not done yet. Class isn't dismissed."

"I have to go to the bathroom."

"Oh, okay. Then come right back."

Inside the big house, a man took her arm. "Aren't you supposed to be outside?

She looked at him, at his odd mustache that was thicker on one side and said, "I'm done with my painting. The teacher said I could come inside."

He started to say something and she interrupted, "The sun's too bright. I'm getting a migraine."

A woman approached them and said to the man, "You're supposed to start the Bingo game in the lounge. They're waiting."

"Be right there." He turned to her and said, "Okay, go to your room. But don't wake up Alice."

She almost spat at him. "I'm not going to wake up Alice! She's been asleep forever. She's probably dead." She headed down the long corridor hung with pictures of residents who had recently died and went right out the front door. She'd lied about the sun being too bright. If anything, it wasn't bright enough.

❋　❋　❋

She has been gone at least two days, she thinks. And one night. She'd eaten the chocolate bar that was in the pocket of her skirt as soon as she left the big house. She'd slept inside a church, on a hard pew. She woke up when she heard singing, a coat that wasn't hers covering her. When the people lined up in the aisle, she did too. The man up front gave her a small, moist cracker. She asked him if she could have another one. His eyes grew large and he shook his head. A woman behind her slipped her hand through her arm and said, "Come with me, dear," but she pushed her away and said, "I don't have to go with you!" She walked out of the church and down a street with lots of cars going past.

She likes the hum of the cars' engines, the rushing sound of air as they pass her. I used to drive, she thinks. I drove Charles to school and I drove to the office. I typed every day. Sometimes I had to use carbon paper and it was so messy. She says, "Now is the time for all good men to come to the aid of the party." I could still type, she tells herself.

The street is wide and lined with stores. Maybe one sells coffee, she hopes. That was a nice thing about the big house; there was always coffee. Her son encouraged her to drink it. "It's supposed to be good for memory," he always said. Once she had snapped back, "Then you drink it!" Maybe more than once.

She walks inside a shop with a large window and says to a man seated in a black vinyl chair mounted on a strange silver pole, "I'd like coffee, please. Cream and one sugar."

He smiles at her and closes the newspaper he's been reading. "I'm sorry, Ma'am. I cut hair."

Her hands fly to her head. She feels her hair, sparse and coarse, and says, "Don't you dare touch my hair!"

"I won't. Don't worry, I won't." He slides off of the chair and stands. "Ma'am, is there someone I can call? Do you need a ride?"

"To where?"

"I don't know. To your house? Do you live near here?"

She shakes her head. "I used to live in a big house. There were too many people. I left." She looks through the window glass. "Is the cemetery near here?"

"Cemetery? No. Ma'am, where do you live?"

He's going to be trouble. She points through the glass door. "Over there. I'm going now." He opens the door for her, saying, "If I can help you with anything, please come back."

She is hungry, so hungry. She walks on until she sees the place with a smiling hamburger on a big sign. She crosses the street and sits at a table outside the restaurant. She sniffs. The scent of grease and salt is heavenly. She is so hungry, she could die. She has no money. The big house people took her money. Thieves. She knows if she demands food at this restaurant, they will call someone from the big house. She puts her head on the table and starts to cry. She realizes her underwear is becoming wet and thinks, I'm crying there, too.

"Ma'am? Ma'am? Here, Ma'am." A man, chubby and short, puts a bag in front of her. "You have to leave after you eat that. Okay?" Despite his size, his teeth are large, his eyeteeth so pointy! The better to eat you with my dear, she thinks, and is too frightened to say thank you before he walks away. She unrolls the folded top of the bag and takes out a warm sandwich wrapped in oily yellow paper and French fries in an open box as red as a fire truck. Next to the bag, God bless him! the man had set a cup of coffee, packets of sugar and a little capsule of cream, the seal already pulled back a bit for her. The food is strange and delicious. A slimy pickle coated with too much mustard sticks to the roof of her mouth. Pushing at it with her tongue, she swallows and then coughs over and over. She waits until her throat finally relaxes, takes a gulp of coffee, and wonders why the man didn't bring ketchup for the French fries. At the big house, there is always ketchup in little bowls on the table, no squeeze bottles. You have to use spoons to put the red sauce on your food. Alice, stupid Alice, thought it was soup one day and ate an entire bowl of it. The big house people then made Alice eat in the special dining room, the small one where young women cut your food and feed it to you. Chewing the last bite of her hamburger, she thinks, I don't ever want to eat there with Alice.

❋   ❋   ❋

She walks and walks and hopes she's going in the right direction. The shops are gone now. She sees houses with driveways, some with cars in them. She comes to a patch of sidewalk with pictures drawn in chalk. On one segment, there is the smiling face of a little girl with squiggly yellow hair that looks like the ramen noodles they sometimes have for lunch at the big house. There are drawings on the sidewalk too, pictures of trees and a cat, or maybe a dog, some four-legged creature with triangular ears. She walks up the driveway and sees that the drawings continue on a small concrete path next to the garage. Rainbows, many of them, thick and thin arches of color that blend in places. She looks at each one of them, taking steps, and comes to the house's backyard.

Is this a backyard? She gasps and covers her mouth. There's another house here, a tiny pale blue house with white shutters around a little window, and a pink door. The roof is a real roof, lovely little slate shingles. She turns to look at the large house in front of the backyard and sees that the shingles match! There's a flower box under the window filled with daffodils. Daffodils! She hasn't seen them in so long. When she bends to inhale their scent, though, they smell like the shower curtain at the big house. She touches what appears to be a delicate blossom but it's firm between her thumb and finger. She turns the doorknob and stoops to enter the tiny house. Once inside, though, she can almost stand up straight. She has to crouch just a bit. She looks about, marveling at the little furniture. There's a wooden rectangular table with two chairs, all painted a soft pink. Puzzle pieces, mostly black, white, and red, are scattered on it. Studying them, she guesses that, if put together, the picture would be of a cow standing near a barn. There's also a somewhat larger rocking chair painted white although the paint is peeling on the arms. There are no lamps but there's plenty of sunshine coming through the window. The walls are made of particleboard and painted pale yellow. The floor, wide wooden slats, is stained a dark, dark brown. So practical, she thinks; it doesn't show the dirt.

She tries to sit on the rocking chair, grasping the arms and lowering herself. The seat is too narrow but, yes, there now, with her legs crossed, she can almost manage. She looks around. Isn't there supposed to be a chair that's too big and a chair that's too small and one just right? With her one foot on the floor, she pushes to make the chair rock and smiles as she closes her eyes. She marvels that her stomach is full and she has found a little house. So little the people in the big house will never find her. She is home.

She must've fallen asleep. When she opens her eyes, a small child is standing in front of her, a little girl with blue eyes and springy blonde curls. She remembers the chalk picture of the girl with ramen noodle hair. Smiling, she says to the child, "Why, hello. How are you?"

When the little girl smiles back and says, "Good," she sees that the child still has all of her baby teeth.

"Well, that's fine, dear. Tell me, what's your name?"

Stepping closer, the little girl puts her hands in the pockets of her dungarees and answers, "Lizzie."

She cups her cheeks with her hands. *Lizzie!*

The girl scratches her cheek and says, "What's your name?"

She leans forward, bringing her face close to the girl's and says, "Guess what? My name is your name."

The girl's eyes expand. "Really?"

Nodding, she blinks to keep tears from slipping down her cheeks. She doesn't want to frighten this little cherub. "Yes, I'm Lizzie, too. Why, when I was your age, my mother used to call me 'Busy Lizzie' because I did so many things. I took dance class and I took elocution lessons. Oh, they don't teach them any more, Sweetie, but they were lessons that taught you to speak well, to project your voice when you were doing a recitation. A recitation of a poem or a speech. Sometimes I'd forget the words. Oh, I would get so mad." Grinning, she clenches her hands and shakes them for effect. "Then my mother would say, 'Lizzie's in a tizzy,' and that made me even madder," she laughs.

Lifting her eyebrows, her chin coming forward, the girl says, "I know the ABCs and I can count to fifty."

"You can?" She opens her mouth widely and flops a hand to her chest.

Proud, the little girl nods and starts to count. When she finishes, the woman claps and says, "Well, *that* was a recitation! A very good one!"

Smiling, the girl says, "I know a lot more than Teddy."

"You have a Teddy bear? You know, I did, too. Actually, I had a whole collection but my favorite was Theodore. He was named for President Theodore Roosevelt."

The girl puts her hands on her hips, saying, "*No*, Teddy is my *brother*. He's two and a half."

"Oh! Thank you for explaining that. And how old are you, Lizzie? A big girl like you, you must be . . ." She lowers her eyebrows to appear to be thinking hard.

"Four!"

"Four! Why you are a big girl, aren't you?"

"Yes. Why are you here?"

She says nothing. Shifting in the chair, she realizes that her hip hurts, that it is pressed up against the arm of the rocker. Finally, she answers, "I came to meet you, Lizzie."

Whispering, the little girl says, "I'm not supposed to talk to strangers. Don't tell Mommy."

She inhales and struggles to stand. "Well, Lizzie, we're not strangers any more and it was so nice to meet you." She stoops to shake the little girl's hand.

Lizzie says, hope in her voice. "I could tell Mommy you're not a stranger. If she knows we have the same name, maybe she won't think you're a stranger."

"Thank you, Lizzie, but your mommy is very wise. We shouldn't talk to strangers. I have to be on my way."

At the door, the woman turns to wave to the little girl. Lowering her head, she steps through the doorway and finds her way around the side of the garage and back onto the sidewalk in front of the house. Squinting in the bright sun, she looks left, then right, before remembering that there's no need to find the cemetery. She knows her name. Elizabeth. When she was little, everyone called her Lizzie. And then, in college, Liz. She has been Liz for so many years although her son calls her, "Mother." She would like to tell him about the tiny house and the girl, little Lizzie. He will be amazed that she has had such an adventure. But how will she find Charles? Oh dear, she thinks, I was supposed to leave a trail of breadcrumbs.

She hears a voice call, "There she is!" Turning, she sees Lizzie with a woman, a tall woman with squiggly hair like Lizzie's but darker, almost brown. The woman is holding a small boy wearing a blue hat that ties under his chin. She looks worried but then mothers often do. Still, the three of them standing there together make such a nice family. In this sunlight, she can see them so clearly.

III. FAMILY

JOAN DOBBIE

WHY I DIDN'T WRITE POEMS

That first summer
of Andy started in May
& just never quit. That luscious,
delicious, fat, golden sun
never let go. All day
day after day, I lay with my new
baby son, my chubby, pink, naked
beautiful peeper, under that sun
that I hadn't yet learned
not to trust, while my just as
naked, just as beautiful, impishly
adorable daughter, my Dawn,
played Barbie, or waded, or
swung on the swings. And I
was almost as naked as they
were, my gorgeous, naked, golden,
sun-drinking, child-swollen breasts
were as big & as full & as fecund
as planets. I made oceans
of milk. I made enough milk
in those days to drown an orphanage
of unwanted children. If I still
had all that milk I could send
truckloads down to San Francisco
to help nourish the homeless. I made
so much milk in those days that
sometimes Andy would choke. I'd
have to back off, my lush, sweet, creamy
thick milk gushing out over the

lawn in two snowy white fountains
feeding the flowering apple tree,
the raspberry bushes, even the
milkweeds themselves got more milk.
The dogs came around to lick off
the grass. Honeybees gathered
& danced for their queen. I was
content as a clover-fed cow & all
of my clovers had four leaves
or more. Of course I didn't
write poems.

ZACK ROGOW

EAGER FOR EACH DETAIL

My daughter, perched on my lap, pleads
for one more bedtime book. I read
with my cheek resting
on her hair, thin and soft as cat fur.

Then she drops the farm
back into its box:
horse, sheep, fence,
the world packaged and put away
till tomorrow.

She kisses her mom goodnight,
just having learned how to smack
her lips, though not always
when they touch the cheek.
I lift her upstairs
as she gazes one last time
over her domain.

I wash every one of her fingers,
and she throws her head back,
giggles wildly when I try to brush her teeth,
howls into her towel
while I pat her lips dry.

Clean cloth diapers.
"Sleeper!" she whoops as I slip
her into it, one limb at a time.
Then we glance at the peach twilight
over the garden as I pull down the shade.
One more hug and too many kisses.

I hoist her into the crib,
her koala, face down on one side of her head,
her dolly dreaming on the other.
My hands mold the blankets around her.
As she shifts under the covers,
looking for that good spot
I close the door behind me
slowly turning the handle back
so it doesn't make a sound.

LEARNING TO BE HAPPY

A parent showing
a small child
I try
to teach myself
to be happy.

Look at the blue sunlight,
I tell myself,
how it rains
onto the green oak leaves, look

at your daughters,
how they look at you
when you swing open the front door
as if unlocking
a huge safe. Lock out

all the voices.
Let your lips
slacken. Float
on your life
as it scoops you up
and rocks you.

Let the ones you love
encircle you
like birthday candles
but still remember
to wish.

PATRICIA BARONE

MAKING BONE LACE

Future rounds the curve of her
downy scalp, her pulsing
vulnerable fontanels.

Restless beneath the emerging
ridges of her cheeks, it raises breasts,
lengthens legs, and even skins her knees.

Lesions heal, a dance of cells.
Light glancing off her sheen of skin, she grows

a memory of fissure in her bones,
preview of the mineral honeycomb she'll be.

The skeleton traceries of leaves,
the way light splinters and reassembles:

"Objects aren't solid—this rock,"
she tells her children, "is holey, full
of space around the worlds
too small for us to see."

Knowing each atom, a whirl of particles,
is holy and each decays,

she isn't surprised when her future comes
already crazed, resembling
a Raku bowl holding one candle.

THE FROZEN LAKE

Our children's voices took on the chirping
quality of sparrows' liquid song.
Their feet rustled leaves, dislodging
stones that clicked and thudded
on the steep and shifting path.

Stan's muscular legs pushed him up
against the pull of gravity,
while I longed to sleep in the meadow
among the lupine and the columbine.

Halfway up the rocky foothills
of the Grand Tetons I climbed
past exhaustion, hearing the faint notes
of my family in the thinner air—
There they were on ice, grassy hummocks,
and teetering on rocks across the frozen stream.

Young, we parents didn't think of bears
or night falling faster through the sunset
than our feet could walk.
The ranger led us down,
as the moon peered over our shoulders.

Stan said to take pictures in our minds' eyes.
We saw our children in each other's eyes
against forget-me-nots in permafrost.

A resounding whirr rose,
the wind through the canyon
filling the shallows with snow.
An ice-wrinkled blue pool pinged
beneath birds' feet.

Frosted branches rubbed together,
a climbing whine that tipped
toward harmony. Pleasing discord
crackled over a glassy meadow's sea.

JENNIFER L. FREED

CITY PARK

and the jonquils singing
yellow yellow yellow
splashing down happy
hills and the spill of violets
beneath birchmapleoak
and the blue jay dart
and the cardinal flash
and the chicka-dee-dee-dee
and iridescent pigeons
peck-pecking under benches
for crumbs of bag-lunching
in magnolia hyacinth air
and two flying boys on blue bicycles
Saturday Dad calling *slow*
down slow down while he
speeds up to catch the wind
in his hair and his boys
rush-tumbling down laughing
laughing into blossoms
budding, blooming
everywhere.

KENNETH WISE

A DAY AT THE BALLPARK

The baseball slowly rolls across the dirt next to home plate and comes to a halt beside the catcher, who picks it up with his bare hand. He turns to the umpire, who straightens up from his squatted position, looks down at the clicker in his hand and says in a barely audible voice, "Ball."

The batter remains frozen. The umpire, who has the lifeless demeanor of a person handing out rental shoes at a bowling alley, points to first base and says, "Take your base." The batter lobs his bat towards his dugout and heads to first. There are players at each base, and in a choreographic fashion, they all slowly jog to the next one. The runner from third steps on home, picks up the bat from the last batter and walks towards the visitor's dugout. He slaps five with the batter on deck, who steps up to hit.

The scoreboard flickers from 5-0 to 6-0. The light that signifies outs cruelly remains unlit. I stand up from the wooden beam that runs across the dugout, wipe the dirt off the seat of my pants and grip the rusty chain link fence that provides protection. This is just the first inning. It already feels like it's endless and, without any outs, it's going to last an eternity. The worst part is that my son is responsible. He has thrown one strike in the last four batters. It's a walkathon.

"Come on, James, just throw strikes." James's hat is pulled down to just above his eyes. The cap creates a shadow over his face, so I can barely make out his expression. He nods to me and steps on the rubber.

James lifts his leg, pulls his arm back and hurls the ball towards the catcher. The ball ricochets off the ground. The batter attempts to avoid it by jumping, but it clips his front foot. The umpire holds his hands up and declares, "Dead ball." He directs the player to go to first. Once again the runners move ahead one base, and the scoreboard flips from 6-0 to 7-0. I close my eyes and massage my forehead.

The head coach for our team, Bill, on the bench with his arms and legs out like he's relaxing at the beach, says to me, "He's really struggling today." Next to Bill is a player, Eric, who is also sitting on the bench. He is creating a pyramid from stones he's gathered from the ground of the dugout. His focus on the construction of his miniature Mayan structure makes him impervious to the events around him.

"I know. He looks great throwing at practice. I don't get it," I say.

"I'll give him some more time. Hopefully he'll come around." Bill says.

I clap my hands and yell to James, "Come on. Get a big leg kick and stay on your powerline."

James nods to me, lifts his leg and fires the ball over the plate. The catcher receives the ball in his glove and freezes, waiting for the call. The umpires stares at the location of the pitch, stands up, lifts his mask off, pulls out a small towel from his back pocket, wipes his face and ponders. He looks like a husband, stuck at Home Depot with his wife, being asked to pick between two color palettes so they can paint the guest room. I look over to James, who awaits his decision like a convict bracing himself for a sentence. "A little low. Ball." The call is a body shot to James's gut. He bends in half and grabs his legs. He stands back up, puts his hands on his head and goes back on the rubber.

A little low! The players are nine years old! My son is floundering out there, and this moron is worried about a few inches. I take a breath, calm myself and yell to the mound, "Good pitch, James. Really good pitch," I say in a slow, loud, deliberate voice so the umpire will know he missed a call. "Just get it up a little higher." James keeps his focus on the plate and delivers another ball. As soon as it leaves his hand, the upper trajectory is evident as it flies well over the head of the catcher and the umpire. The scoreboard operator, sitting in a wooden structure above home plate, ducks for cover as the ball smashes into the wood directly below her. The umpire remains fixed in his position and says, "Ball."

I take my hat off and rest my head on the fence. This is terrible. I scan the field. The second baseman has both arms extended and spins in circles while slowly releasing dirt from his ungloved hand into the air. He appears to be sending some sort of distress signal to overhead aircraft. Third base is talking to the runner on base, and centerfield is turned sideways, staring off into the distance. I yell, "Come on, guys, baseball ready. Someone make a play!" None of the players bother to respond.

The third base coach from the other team claps his hands and says to the batter, "Be ready for a fastball. Let it travel and drive it." The batter takes a practice swing and steps back into the box.

"James, just pretend like we are playing catch in the front yard. I'm going to walk you through this, and we're going to throw a strike together. I want you to get your arm back all the way like you're showing the ball to second base." James pulls his arm back. "Good, now I want you to bring it over top and release the ball by your ear." I'm walking him through this in such detail I feel like I'm a 911 operator talking someone through an emergency tracheotomy. He follows along. When his hand gets to his ear, I yell, "Now let it fly." The ball travels straight and true. The batter's eyes grow twice in size. He swings the bat and makes contact. The ball rolls on the ground towards third base. The player on third is still talking to the opposing runner.

I scream, "Mason, field the ball!"

Mason's head snaps to where the ball is. He puts his glove down to scoop up the grounder, but it rolls under his legs. He spins in a circle, locates the ball, picks it up with his bare hand and holds it up like it's a prize. The runner on third easily makes it home, and the runners all advance.

"Tag the base," I scream.

Mason registers what I'm saying and moves towards the bag, but it's too late. The runner coming from second to third is safe.

The scoreboard flips, 8-0.

Bill comes over to me. "I'm going to talk to James and tell him if he can't strike this next kid out, I'm going to pull him. I have a dinner reservation tonight, and the way this is going, I'm going to have to cancel." He leaves the dugout, signals to the umpire for time and makes it to the mound. He puts his arm around James and coaches him. Bill steps away, illustrates a throwing motion and continues to talk.

My mind drifts back to when James was a toddler, and we would go for walks every night after dinner. Just the two of us. We would wander through the neighborhood, go to a small stream and he would throw rocks into it. I would lead him home, give him a hug and put him into bed. I miss those days. When he was that age, I dreamed he would be a straight A student and a great athlete. I didn't see myself in a dirty dugout begging him to lob a ball over the plate or at his school having his teacher tell me her "concerns about his transposition of letters when reading."

I look around towards the parents, who are whispering to each other. This isn't just a personal failure. It's public. He's out there bouncing one ball on the ground after another, and there is nothing I can do to help him. I'm not some professional coach that would have some idea about a flaw in his mechanics. After telling him the two minor points I know about throwing, I have nothing else to offer.

I so badly would want to be able to say or do something so that he could be successful here. Some of these kids are so good. They show up with their fabulous parents in their fabulous cars, which have stickers from their fabulous college. They get out holding their double Frappuccinos with no foam whip and relax in the shade while their fabulous kids strike everyone out and hit the ball over the fence. Then they go home and watch their fabulous college win a big football game and post it all on Facebook. The college I went to didn't even have a football team. Our homecoming was a soccer game, and we always lost.

I wish James was like those kids. I wish that we could just show up here, and he would dominate, and I wouldn't be filled with stress and anxiety every time he plays. It's just another reminder how everything is so damn hard. Work, family, attending all the million activities kids have to do nowadays. It's all so exhausting. Sometimes I feel like I could close my eyes and sleep for days.

Bill slaps James on the back, puts his hands in his pockets, wanders to the dugout and stands next to me. He keeps his vision focused on the field and says, "I told him he had to get this guy out, or I was going to pull him."

"Okay," I say and then yell to James, "Come on, buddy. Let's go."

James winds up and hurls the ball to the catcher. The umpire yells, "Strike one."

The ball returns to James, who delivers another laser right to the catcher. "Strike two."

"Alright James, now you're on track."

James pulls back and throws another gem. The umpire punches out the batter.

Bill holds up his index finger to the team. "One down. Play is at any base."

The next batter steps into the box. James takes a deep breath and throws a pitch. The batter makes contact, and the ball sails into the outfield between left and center field. The left fielder scoops the ball off the ground and throws it in the general direction of the infield. All of the runners are on the move as the shortstop picks up the ball, turns and holds it in a throwing position. He pumps towards first base but realizes it would be too late for that and throws it towards home. The ball is off target and ends up midway between home and first and in front of the dugout. If the fence wasn't here, I could reach down and grab it. The catcher runs towards where the ball is but can't locate it. I stick my finger through the webbing of the fence and point to the ball. "Pick it up!" I yell. He grabs the ball and goes to throw it to the infield. "No," I scream. "Run it back to the pitcher." The catcher holds the ball up, takes it to James and drops it in his glove. The scoreboard flips over to 10-0.

Bill shakes his head, walks up to the mound, pats James on the head and yells to the dugout, "Come on, Eric." Eric lifts his head, knocks over his art project, picks up his glove and jogs to the mound. James makes his way to the dugout and sits on the bench.

This is my fault. My son is born with the genetic stain of my mediocrity. Everything he'll do will be difficult. School, girls, sports. None of it will come easily or naturally. He'll be awkward on and off the field and will always be a spectator of people who can somehow just float by in life. He'll spend his life congratulating them for their success while rarely having any of his own.

I made him do this. I told him that I played baseball and that he had to. I didn't drag him into the sport, but I did make him participate. If it wasn't for me, he wouldn't have been out here, and this humiliation wouldn't have happened. I set him up to fail, and now he's probably crushed by it and will never want to play again. This defeat will scar him, and he'll never try anything for fear that something like this will happen to him again.

I walk over to him. He sits with his head down staring at his feet. I'm going to put my arm around him and let him know that he can fail, and I'll still love him. I'll always love him. Even if he isn't the greatest player or student or whatever everyone expects him to be, I'll always be his Dad, and we'll always have each other. This is an opportunity to let him know my unconditional support for him. I might not be great at anything else in life, but I can do this. I can comfort my son. I sit next to him, put my arm around him and say, "Hey buddy."

He lifts his head and looks me in the eyes. This is it. He's going to break down. I have to be strong for him. I can't let him know how much I'm hurting for him.

"Dad."

"Yes, James?"

He takes his eyes off me, leans forward and stares into the distance then returns his eyes to mine. His face breaks out into a wide smile, and he says, "Did you see me strike that guy out?" He has the mouth of a hockey player with uneven teeth and empty gaps.

I'm jolted by his response. His smile smashes all the fears I was conjuring for my son and brings me back to the reality that this isn't about some abstract construction I created about an athletic ideal. This is about spending time as a father and son. Every instant of time that we are here is a piece of life that we can never get back, and wasting it worrying about my own and other people's expectation robs us of savoring these precious moments.

"After we get ice cream, can we practice pitching at home? I want to strike more guys out," he says.

"Who said we were getting ice cream?"

"We always get ice cream after games." He leans back into my chest.

"We do?"

"We did last game, so now it's a tradition."

"We can get ice cream and practice pitching," I tell him, chuckling at his logic.

We sit holding each other. We don't talk; we just embrace and silently share our love for each other. I look out to the field and watch the shortstop overthrow first base, all the batters move and the scoreboard flickers to an even more outsized lead. The first baseman runs over to the fence to pick up the ball. On the other side of the fence sits an open trash can with flies swarming over the garbage that rots in the summer heat. The dugout is covered with a film of dust that is embedded into every inch of the space. The team's gear and water bottles are in piles all around me. Sitting here among this mess and holding my son, I realize that he's still the little boy I took to the stream to throw rocks, and I'm still the dad holding his hand and bringing him home. It strikes me that many times our greatest moments of joy are found in the most unexpected places at the most unexpected times.

LAURIE KLEIN

FROM THE CUCKOO CLOCK ROOM
(after W. S. Merwin)

Thank you my scariest day
in the middle of almost being
un-adopted by Aunt Irene
Thank you that both of us hiccup
a lot which makes us laugh
and can change a mind
She says my hair's just like
the minnowy stream out back
that forgets where it's going
Thank you tortoiseshell hairbrush
and rocking chair
Thank you six locks on our door
ever since Mr. Zoniger's missing wife
shot their mailbox to bits
Now he eats in our kitchen
Four o'clock Cuckoo reminds me
to run Mr. Z's dog around
singing Thank you red leather leash
looped around my glove like a hug
and down at the basset-hound end
that silver thingummy strong as teeth
or a promise written in cursive
that says I can stay I can stay
Afterward when I kneel down lucky
I unclip his waggery self and
flakes of his skin fall on my sleeve
like every star a kid ever wished on

ROSEMARY VOLZ

MR. BUSCEMI'S MIRROR

Jacaranda, Chinaberry sound sweet
In the ear, feel good on the tongue,
But they are not my trees, not my words.
June bugs on screen door, yellow light on low pines,
Belong in the family album of somebody else.

I remember Earl Gafney's blue Plymouth,
And how he always parked it under the streetlight
So that the metallic paint would sparkle and catch
The eye of a twelve-year-old girl looking
Through lace curtains on a moonless night.
And on the hood was a metal ornament
Shaped like the top half of a naked lady,
A chromium Madonna with breasts like bullets.
And if I felt lonely enough (which I usually did),
I was that silver lady and Earl's car was moving like thunder
Through the streets of Brooklyn, my nipples were slicing
The hot breath of the city as my polished hair flowed past
The empty lots of Pitkin Avenue and my greedy iron lips parted
To reveal a cherry-coke voice screaming, "Faster, Faster!"

And even before that, I remember Mr. Buscemi's Barber Shop,
Going there with mother and Andrew on stony winter afternoons.
Andrew fat legs dangling from a wooden booster seat
As I sat next to a hissing radiator
And mother thumbed through magazines
And sighed at things she'd never own.
The barber's scissors clipping the air,
Black combs bobbing in blue water

As my brother's black ringlets floated down
To white tiles and I waited, waited
For Mr. Buscemi to take out that special brush,
And sweep the hairs from Andrew's neck,
And the ones he'd miss, he'd blow off.
A yellow canary singing in a bamboo cage,
A potted palm filtering the dying sunlight,
And my wide eyes growing weary because
They did not know what was more beautiful to watch,
The real thing or their reflection in Mr. Buscemi's mirror.

CHARISSA MENEFEE

MOVING THE VASE

Sometimes I drive my mother crazy,
moving little things around in the house,
but she has to admit that things look
better where I put them, that it's
where they always belonged.

One time she saw me looking at this vase,
the skinny blue one with the white flowers.
She said, *Don't move that.*
And I said, *I have to.*
And she said, *Don't you dare move that!*

I grabbed it before she could stop me, shoved
it across the table to where I knew it had to be.
I don't know why I couldn't mind her, what
comes over me when I have to fix something.
It's like I'm not in control.

Even her walk was mad, when she came over to
shift the vase to its original spot, but then she
looked at me, sighed and shook her head,
because she could see now that it belonged there,
but she couldn't see it until I helped her.

MY PARENTS MEET

She sits in the student union
with her date, a shy boy
from chemistry class.

My father sprawls onto the couch
opposite them, stretches his
cowboy-booted legs onto the
coffee table, and stares.

After the boy from chemistry
breaks into a sweat, excuses
himself for a moment—

My father tips back his black hat,
says, it's now or never, and she
takes his hand, because now
seems like a pretty good gamble.

MY GRANDMOTHER DREAMS
SHE IS SEWING

Her wheelchair finally outside in the sun's warmth,
the memory returns to her arthritic fingers, the
needle's rhythm, the textures of cloth, buttons, thread.

My grandmother dreams she is sewing, the whirr
of the machine, pressing the pedal, feeding the fabric,
the stitches linking deftly as she turns the cloth at
precisely the right moment—a perfect corner.

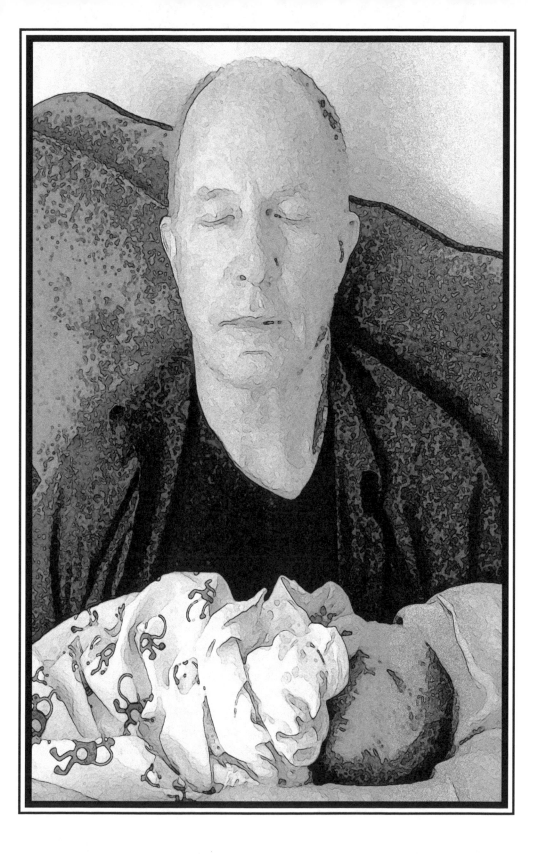

DEBORAH A. SCHMEDEMANN

GLORY

10:00 Sunday morning, July 5th, 2015, the north side of Chicago: the city is waking up and warming up. My husband and I enter the century-old church and settle in to worship.

Although I have never been here before, this sanctuary is familiar space. Beams stained deep walnut crisscross its high, white-washed ceiling. The pews of well-worn oak flank a still-plush rose carpet. The sun filters through stained-glass windows depicting New Testament scenes. Two ranks of organ pipes frame the altar, into which is carved "Heilig, Heilig, Heilig"—Holy, Holy, Holy in German, the language of my forbearers. I am a mixed-brand Christian: baptized by an Episcopalian Army chaplain, raised Presbyterian by parents with Baptist and Lutheran roots, married to a one-time United Church of Christ pastor, sometimes a Methodist, now a member of a U.C.C.-Presbyterian church. Yes, this place says "church" to me.

Soon, I am swept along into the service celebrating our nation's birthday under God. I recite familiar liturgy, listen to familiar scriptures, nod to familiar themes in the sermon. I rise in accord with the asterisks in the bulletin. With others, I sing out familiar verses as the organ hums along: "Our country 'tis of thee, sweet land of liberty."

❄   ❄   ❄

Almost twenty-four hours ago, I met the new love of my life. Swaddled in a blanket of white printed with blue lions, this newborn was resting, pink head against bared breastbone, in the arms of his mother, my older daughter Mary. Mary had given birth to this baby boy at 1:39 a.m. on July 4th, and she and her husband Adam had named their baby, my first grandchild, Luke.

When I took Luke from Mary, I gazed first at his rounded rosy head, capped in delicate brown strands. His big eyes peered back, blue-brown and unflinching. His nose commanded attention. My first words about the new love of my life? "Gee, he has a really big nose." His pouty lower lip looked like a tulip petal. He was alert as could be, rested still against my chest, and gave off an air of disgruntlement and curiosity. His shoulders and arms too were clothed in delicate brown strands (Adam: "He's a beast!"), and his pink hands curled into loose fists. Newborn though he was, he seemed somehow familiar.

So, I thought, *we finally meet.* Intuitively, I had known of this baby boy for nine months. I am not a mystical person; indeed, most would describe me as analytical and practical; I was a lawyer and law professor for over three decades. And yet: I had a dream about Luke's conception about the time he was, in fact, conceived. And about two months before his birth, when no one knew his gender and his parents had not revealed their choices of names, it came to me, as I jogged, that Mary would bear a boy on July 4th and name him "Luke."

As I held Luke in my arms that first time, my emotions were a spicy stew. I was awe-struck at his mere being: he was, as all newborns I have ever cradled, a testimony to life beginning and an embodiment of innocence. I was grateful to be alive for this moment: my wonderful mother died when I was a teenager, and in my deepest being I have never expected to experience milestones that she missed. I was relieved that all had gone well: Mary had planned on a home birth, only to discover as she was about to deliver that the baby was in breech presentation, requiring an ambulance trip to the hospital. I was pleased—yes, proud—that my strong and determined daughter had pulled off a natural breech delivery of such a big baby (eight and a half pounds—oof!).

Yet, deep down, I was melancholy: it was July 4th, and I missed my patriot.

✳   ✳   ✳

One-eighth of little Luke's genes trace back to Keith Schmedemann: my father, Mary's grandfather, Luke's great-grandfather. One day, Luke will learn that I kept my maiden name when I married out of devotion to my father; that Mary's original last name, Bowmann, was formed from parts of her father's last name (Bower) and mine; and that Mary gave Luke that same name, Bowmann, as his middle name. Although linked through a few letters, Keith and Luke never overlapped in life: Keith died at ninety-three in 2013, over two years before Luke was born.

Thus Luke would never hear my father speak in his trademark "colonel's voice." My father came of age during the Great Depression, and he began his U.S. Army career through officer training in college. During World War II, he landed at Normandy Beach the day after D-Day, fought through the Battle of the Bulge, and contributed to the liberation of the Jewish internment camp at Buchenwald. He led a battalion during the Korean Conflict. He spent my pre-school years commanding an infantry battle group in West Germany during the Cold War. Returning stateside, he served several tours of duty in the belly of the Pentagon, sorting out matters of too much war and too little peace into the Vietnam years.

Off-duty, this soldier was Daddy to two daughters. I am the one cast in his mold: his physical carbon copy (gender aside), the inheritor of his curly hair and migraine headaches, his partner in pursuing public service, a fellow fan of long bike rides and evening dog walks, a kindred connoisseur of well-written prose and bad puns. He was Smitty; I became Schmed.

My father's colonel's voice is the motif in the soundtrack of my memory. When I was a child, my father was the superintendent of our church school. He would stand before us—just over six feet tall, ramrod straight and trim; attired in a classic navy suit with crisp white shirt and striped tie; bald already in his forties with soft brown eyes—and deliver a children's message. When we were rambunctious, he would call out "Children!" in his colonel's voice, and we would settle right down, responding to his voice of calming authority.

His colonel's voice sounded somberly when I was in my teens. In the late 1960s and early 1970s, the country was ripping itself apart in the streets and on the nightly news, over civil wrongs, economic injustice, an unwinnable war. I was fascinated, appalled, scared. My father talked openly with me and my sister about the issues of the day, about our precious country, about our responsibility to make our country better. His was a voice of moral imperative.

As we lived our adult decades together, I became most fond of the mellower timbre of my father's voice. After the death of my mother and his second wife as well, as we sat in church pews together, he would take my hand when it came time to recite the Lord's Prayer. We always used the traditional phrasing, "Our Father," no "Mother" or "Creator" for us. ("Our Father" it is for me, still.) My father proclaimed this prayer—no mumbling for him. His was a voice of firm faith.

As I became a lawyer, law professor, and mother, I sought to find my own compelling voice. Sometimes I thought that I needed to work on my timbre, my enunciation. I eventually figured out, of course, that my father's colonel's voice had little to do with these things and more to do with what propelled his voice: the life lived, the experiences embedded, the lessons learned.

✳   ✳   ✳

As the service nears its end on July 5th in the Chicago church, the organ heralds a familiar tune, the Battle Hymn of the Republic: "Mine eyes have seen the glory of the coming of the Lord." This was my father's favorite hymn. The congregation rises around me. But I sit, still, in the pew as I hear something for the first time since my father's death two years earlier. It is *his* rich baritone singing "the glory of the coming of the Lord" over my right shoulder. Just eight words, but they are enough. Tears flow down my cheeks.

They are tears of release,—no, of *joy* and realization. I realize that little Luke, *familiar* Luke, resembles my father—no surprise, really, given that Luke's mother is cast in my mold just as I was cast in my father's. I realize that a through-line runs from my father through me and my daughter to this baby boy; the past continues into the future through this boy. And I realize, through my father's voice singing over my shoulder, that *I* now have a glorious responsibility: to give voice to my father's legacy for the next generation.

LORI LEVY

GOOD HEALTH, GRANDMA STYLE

I'll pass on push-ups and pilates.
Walking would be fine—but I can't commit to briskly,
nor to thirty minutes five times a week,
the magic dosage for good health.
Just let me do the floor routine—sit down, get up,
again, again, whenever I am wanted:
the grandma-come-and-play exercise.
Jogging's not for me, but I'll dash back and forth
from kitchen to table twenty times a day,
bringing the little ones whatever they desire,
mostly apple juice or chocolate milk
and cheese and ketchup sandwiches.
I don't need to exercise: I burn calories in the driveway,
just watching them go speeding on their tricycles.

Meditation to relieve life's stress? Yes, if it means
lying on the carpet listening to my grandson,
who hums Batman tunes while building with his Lego.
Mindfulness? I focus, not on breathing, but on her,
my granddaughter, who sings a commentary on her moves.
I'm with her, fully present, as she sets her Lego girls
inside the house she's built
and gives them ice cream cones and cupcakes.

The youngest one, a baby, four-months-old,
turns her head towards me and smiles,
as if she holds the key to my core:
my inner calm, my equilibrium.
I reach my arms out to receive her.
This stretch is all the yoga I require.

ALISON STONE

SHINE

Drifting down from birdfeeders my daughters painted,
pooled at the base of valentines—I find
glitter everywhere. Sparkling between one girl's toes,
on my fingers after snapping a bright
clip into her hair. Stray specks
glint on my cheek, my husband's eyebrows. Twinkle
from the cat's fur. Between the laundry and
the squabbles, I pause,
delight in tiny flecks of gold and silver flinging
light to every corner of my blessed, ordinary life.

IV. INTIMACY

ZACK ROGOW

FRENCH QUARTER

Wasn't that the dream that night on Bourbon Street
when we infiltrated a schmaltzy piano bar
in an old French blacksmith's forge
its walls still black from the blast of the fire
and the tipsy queen dressed in a white suit and boa
like the ghost of Tennessee Williams
gave you his river of feathers
coiling it over you
so you formed a double helix
around the lamppost on St. Philip
while you mugged for that shot
and didn't we literally
dance in the street that night
outside every Zydeco salsa Cajun fluorescent jazz bar
you swaying with that relaxed upward-glancing smile
till I knew this love would go nowhere
was completely impossible
without these moments
so incandescent
they melt down every pre-dawn doubt

FELICIA MITCHELL

JOY IN THE AFTERNOON

There were as many birds
as there were words

the afternoon we sat and listened:
each sound a new sound

or a little more of the same.
And then the rain came

and then the rain went
and the two of us kept talking,

birds here and birds there
and one turkey feather in a jar.

ROSEMARY VOLZ

WONDER

I woke up this morning and the
Gold and purple tree from
Last night's dream was
Blooming on my front lawn.

I ran for the train and
My right knee didn't hurt at all.
It was 8:22 and the 8:15 Express
Was waiting for me.

I reached into my pocket for the ticket
And found my lost keys and a gold doubloon.
A window seat was empty and
A copy of tomorrow's paper was left behind.

The conductor handed me a cup of coffee
And a silver bowl filled with grapes,
So I sat back and watched
Seven corpulent angels cavorting on clouds.

The day was uneventful until I came home
And wonders of wonders,
You were there,
Waiting,
Smiling.

LOWELL JAEGER

GNATS IN LOVE

Late evening and we're winding our way,
my wife and I, up the path from the lake.
Is that fog? my wife says, pointing at our home
on the hillside above us. Both of us blink
and stare. *Can't be,* I say. Not the season.

Still, an eerie haze has inexplicably descended,
enshrouding the entire structure, reducing
roof and windows and doors to a single gauze
apparition, alive in slant sunlight, roiling with incandescent
neon blues and greens as if boiled

from a cauldron. My wife takes my hand,
edges closer, and we stand uncertain, more
awestruck than afraid. It's something
frightfully beautiful, other-worldly, strange. It's moving,
slowly, south along the lakeshore, till it's gone.

In its wake, billions of bodies, each no bigger
than a speck, piles of them—spent bugs—fallen in drifts
around the foundation, peppered across our windowsills.
Well, now we're abuzz with an appreciation for small things.

We fetch a magnifying glass and whisper, push our noses
closer. The tiny wings quiver when we breathe nearby.

ALISON STONE

WHO WOULD'VE THOUGHT

The wind goosebumps our damp
skin as we lie entwined near the pond

listening to fish splash and the crickets'
din. After kids and cranky

sleep-deprived years, still the
dim, cloud-veiled stars dazzle. Dark

earth breathes beneath us as our
aging bodies wake and feed.

CLAUDIA VAN GERVEN

THE GRAND STAIRCASE
Escalante, Utah, 2002

We descend into the river-cut canyon, air crisscrossed
with dragonflies, so hot it glistens

like sheets of water in the distance. We step
gingerly around the prickly pear, opening

outrageous blossoms, the exact color
of pink champagne,

the afternoon brimming giddy as a holiday.
We stop, snap

Photos of blue gentian, scarlet mallow, the way
Indian varnish cascades down canyon walls.

We forget our limbs
are no longer young, the extra pounds we carry.

We forget we are two aging suburbanites
Hiking through an ordinary

marriage, shadows and heat tangled
across a common trail.

We scrabble up a small hillock to read
three solemn figures etched in cliff face

by people we cannot name
but who, for reasons of their own, chiseled this curly

horned goat, this man with antlers brandishing his spear,
these chevrons, we gloss as water, then disappeared

into surmises. At the end of the trail is a waterfall
and a green-blue pool so cold

it will scald our bare-feet, make us whoop
with the icy sweet pain of its clarity.

But we are not there yet.
We are still on the trail, following its coils

through thickets of willow. A hummingbird
nearly collides with sweat-stained raffia

of my hat. He is gone before I can call to you.
We keep ascending, though we can't say why

and the trail wanders off in tangles of gambrel oak.
Our boots keep moving through the dazzle

Of brilliant weather where a young red-tailed hawk
blazes, screaming with joy, her wings nuzzling

the hot upthrust of a thermal, black eyes igniting as she
scans dusty hard pan for tiny black spoor

of rabbits that skitter, skitter of voles. Dirt drifts
up from the trail, a fine red powder we breathe in.

It covers our faces, marks the ridges where time
Has eroded our favorite expressions.

We will read later that this rich ocher dirt is colored
by coal fires that burn

beneath the surface of sage and juniper forest,
that in places we can feel its shimmer under our feet,

a whole strata of fire buried deep in the earth
we've already walked over.

PATRICK CABELLO HANSEL

LOVE POEM
After Billy Collins

You are the cardinal's desire
singing me awake at 4 a.m.
You are the maple in our front yard,
waiting for the sun to run its sap.
You are the hum of the furnace,
cheery in its robust wheezing, but

I can't tell if you are
my wife or my God,
which is profoundly scary,
but also nice to know
I can ask either you
for a hug, and you will—
almost always—say yes.

I sit on the cold front porch
wrapped in a blanket and hot tea
and count the ways grey skies
change on a late winter day:
one...................................,
OK, the houses do not change
either, except for the light
in their eyes that comes on,
goes off, comes on higher up
or lower down, winking
as if to say, "I see you
and I don't mind." I can

hear you moving around upstairs,
your steps from room to room,
the way your body catches
then releases the hundred year
boards. It is like the quietest
form of thunder: no lightning,
no damaging winds, just
the bit of wonder that air
makes when it forgets itself.

The dog's slow barking
wakes my brain just enough
to know I am alive. There is
a taste of brown sugar and
silence in the back of my throat,
where words are born and
quickly fly. We are together
a far country, where distance
is an eyelash and longing a peach.
We watch for the ripening, one
glance at a time, like ravenous birds.

DON THACKREY

MY WINTER SUN

As when the sun relieves the chilled dawn's grey
And choreographs the sparkling in the snow,
So Helen's morning glance provides a ray
Of light that gives our home a gentle glow.

I don't know why this earth-bound angel smiles
When payments on our debts are in arrears;
We missed our ranching goals this year by miles,
And botulism hit our herd of steers.

Our middle son is prey to alcohol,
The baby seems to have a lung disease,
The twins at school face trouble for their brawl
With toughs who ended up with injuries . . .

But still, despite all woes I might compile,
My Helen daily warms me with her smile.

FRANK SALVIDIO

AGAIN

I am too old to be in love again,
Yet all the ancient symptoms reappear:
Her red-gold hair; the sudden heartbeat when
I hear her name; the urge to be there where
I know she'll be; and then to say her name
Again—again!— just as a schoolboy does
Who falls in love at sight. It's all the same,
With everything again just as it was.
But it's ridiculous to want to hold
Her hand; even to think I could would be
Preposterous—absurd—and far too bold
For someone of my years. I cannot see
What this new adolescence can presage,
Except that I'm in love—and at my age!

PATRICIA BARONE

YOUR EYES POSSESSED THE ENDLESS SPACE
in memory of Stan

Breathless on the Jüngfraujoch's high saddle,
I held our baby in a pouch strapped to my breast.
My eyes were focused on you,
trusting the way you carved a gentle turn
into the mountain's side, the sheer drop-off road.

"Mönch, Eiger, and Jüngfrau," you intoned
relishing the mountain peaks' names in your mouth,
even more than the *spargeln*, white asparagus
with Hollandaise sauce, a spring treat.

As we ate, you followed a sun-blessed golden eagle,
her wing span wider than you were tall,
who alighted only to feed her young.

Sitting on the top of Europe, you traced rivers
and lakes marking cantons, Bern and Luzern,
and the sun sank into massifs.

Your happiness became mine, a sort of ecstasy
when far stars, one by one, winked on.
Even extinguished fires
marking the death of worlds.

The moon lighted our future faces—
all luminous forever, just as you are.

RUTH MARGOLIN SILIN

RESURRECTION

I tracked the wind and heard
the moans of grief, tears falling
into a well black and deep.

Then I remembered his touch, his words,
his breath, and all I knew of love and dreams
still mine to hold and keep.

I turned from dark and saw the sunlight filter
through blackened groves to waken sleeping
creatures, light the moving earth and
lift me weightless, free.

PURPOSE

Born with the end in sight even
as the cord is cut.
Enter with a cry, leave with a gasp,
bodies piled into heaps of ash, dust,
pain torn from shredded albums.
To what purpose? I ask
The fuss, the bother of it all.
          And yet . . .
that first time I saw you walking on the beach,
hair blowing, your smile locked with mine,
first sight, first touch, love described
by bards whose pens burn passion
into words, I read you in their songs and
breathe the breath of love.

I NOW PRONOUNCE YOU...

Did we really need to hear those words
to make us legal?
Two of us with 99 years of marriage
wed to others— left solitary, bereft.

Ah, loneliness, a sad and graying word that
creeps upon the psyche and robs the world
of joy?

What did it take to move the clouds,
warm our blood, bring back our mirth?
A meeting of eyes, a stirring within, memories
of flesh upon flesh.

I believe in marriage, he said,
so we spoke our vows, framed the words and
shared our ice cream from a single dish.

V. THE QUOTIDIAN

JENNIFER L. FREED

ABUNDANCE

When your husband has been ill,
when you have just come from the lawyer's
to update your will,
when you have bought and put away
the groceries, and brought down all the children's
laundry, and at last hung up the phone
from the obligatory call to hope
the chatty neighbor's surgery went well,
when it is time to step into the heat
of backyard garden, where the drooping leaves of summer
squash are telling you their thirst,
and you have wished again
the hose your neighbor's son mowed a gash across last weekend
had already been replaced,
then,
as you stand at the spigot once,
then twice,
then thrice,
waiting
for the weighty fullness
in the plastic can,
the slowness
of the chore becomes a loosening
of time,
and so you take the time
to pull up weeds,
to pinch off extra growth of leaves,
and that is how you find the summer's first
tomatoes, like an unexpected gift—

three red and perfect cherries
amidst all the green,
and you pluck them all at once into one palm,
and you allow yourself
to eat them—one, two, three
warm bursts of sun and earth
against your tongue,
and the scent of green has gone into your hands,
and the wind is in the tops of trees,
and a hummingbird is hovering in the Russian Sage,
and you stand very still,
and
breathe.

BALM

It is worth it
to her, lugging the heavy wicker
up from the basement.
In green light, she notices
buzz of cicadas, circling of hawk. Bees
nestling in catmint, sage.
She knows the length of air
will stiffen towels, jeans,
and doesn't care.
She likes watching, from the kitchen window,
how sunlight alters color,
pushes shadow
along draping cloth.
Later,
folding sheets against her chest,
she inhales.
How do you name this? The balm
of doing what your grandmother did. Of knowing
this scent, fresh
off the line.

ALISON STONE

BIRD

It's hard to write about happiness
without sounding smug, dumb,
Hallmarky, derivative, dishonest.
Just as doggerel threatens,
suffering swoops in to rescue you,
take you back to the land
of quirky, black-clad unfortunates,
the familiar smoky bar or tense bedroom.
Velvet Underground on the stereo.
Stale cake in the fridge. So many
metaphors for hunger.
So many slammed doors.
Your obsessive lugubriousness
cooler than the silly leap
your trite heart made this morning
when, tossing balls for the dog,
you looked up and saw a finch whose
yellow feathers gleamed so brightly,
you swelled with ordinary,
it's-been-said-already joy.

FELICIA MITCHELL

BOURRÉE WITH GOLDFINCH

In the morning,
I threw sunflower seeds
onto the porch
and left them there,
temperature dropping,
as I did my chores.
Sweeping, dusting,
washing—it was all a dance,
the dance I do at home
alone with chores.
As cold as it was,
I took compost outside.
It was for the earth or the crows,
whichever took it first,
and also for me,
a reason to stand at a bare beech
that towered over me
and look up.
Later, dusting piano keys,
I began touching them,
one and then the other,
until I sat down with a bourrée
Bach wrote for his children.
It was simple and sweet,
and it made a goldfinch pause
just outside the window
as I played a dance
even birds can dance to.
The goldfinch stayed

until I started a minuet,
a faster tempo lifting its wings,
and then I got up to vacuum.

LORI LEVY

MORNING WALK

The point is to focus.
I could begin with my socks. Texture. Weave.
Thickness of cotton against the bottoms of my feet.
My mind pulls me this way and that way
like a frisky dog yanking at its leash.
Why socks? it wants to know. Why heels, toes
when a single red geranium hangs from a balcony
on a brown stucco building across the street?
And why a single bloom when faced with such abundance
of color and scent? Jasmine, white roses, lemon trees, oranges.
How can I concentrate on the bright, pocked skin
of the fruit on those branches? I am thirsty. I prefer to imagine
orange juice, ice, a tall glass of coldness
I can hold in my hand. So delicious to invent. To drift away
to the *not* here, to glasses I can almost hear clinking
at a party I wasn't at—in a Greek restaurant
where my son played guitar.

Back to socks, shoes pressing down, shadows on the pavement
of ficus leaves. Adirondack chairs beckon
from porches and lawns, always in twos,
always empty, tempting me to sit and
rest for a while. I am thirsty, this city is thirsty,
yards yellowing in L.A., some almost bald.
More and more landscapes of gravel and wood chips,
cactus, deer grass. Whatever will survive.

Is focus the point? Or is it something else?
I thank my socks for taking me on this journey.
For cushioning, absorbing. For being what they are:
soft and white, like the roses I pass—
and worn in places, like the paint on the picket fences.

PINK BERRIES

Is it you who've changed or I?
Now I want to thank you, Ma—
you who knows how to look
at dry brown grass, thorny bushes,
who walks with delight through chaparral,
pointing to the tiny pink berries
on a dull green shrub beside the trail.

You, Ma, who knows the value of a pause—
an hour's nap in the early afternoon,
a cup of coffee savored while the mind floats
cloud-like somewhere else;
a moment of inertia when eyes soak in
the way a gull blends in
to a rock above the cove;

who takes the time to linger
over garlic, basil, olive oil;
over mustache, wrinkles, glass of wine
in a painting of a man on A Night Out.
It's you who reads the tilt
of his head. You
who sees the fervor in his eyes.

BREAKFAST ON THE BALCONY

Yes, I've come for ancient walls and olive trees,
violinists on cobbled streets, old stones
glowing pink in the late afternoon light—
but also for a lumpy sofa and a bowl of grapes,
medley of onions and laughter in stairways,
radios wailing through apartment walls.
And for this, my friend, just as it is:
your little balcony on the fourth floor
where a table stands among empty flowerpots,
broom, pails, boxes, and underpants
pinned to a clothesline with bras and towels—just right
when you dress it with sunflowers
printed on a white cloth and bring out the tray
laid with napkins and silverware, yogurt,
fresh orange juice, coffee, toast and jam.
Lovely, sipping mugs while the sun shines
on TV antennas and geraniums,
rugs hanging over railings, and windows
holding the beginnings of stories.
What more could I ask for
than a chair at your bright yellow table,
high as clear skies, pine trees,
and the dusty red roofs of Jerusalem.

MARK TARALLO

NEAR THE EXXON STATION

Despite the heat the day was so shy and unassuming,
barely able to present itself,
not interested in anything showy,
with countless smiles for the good-intentioned.

There were cars turning every which way—
ridiculous,
the supermarket staked a claim in our hearts.
But it is that boring stretch I am interested in,
a vague memory of a BP or Hess tank billboarded
along the road,
an insignia green like the grass
and the highway sidewalks which go unwalked for days,
driving slowly around the bend
with what you see more familiar than what you left behind.

It's like those middle distances between longing and rejection—
there lies a kind of half-assed wondering.
There is a whiff of waste
and the contemptible idea that it is not too late.
A week there and you could lose yourself,
but I'm interested, I guess,
in most anything that wears its insignificance on its sleeve.

After all, I once walked on a moon-under-sea
with an ethicist from Poland, & it turned into an illuminating conversation
about my high school years.
It seemed that the bits of snow around us
and the landscape which kept switching from shade to sun

had a hand in shaping my opinions
in a quietly comical way, giving them weight they otherwise
wouldn't have had.

So I hold on to that scene
near the Exxon station, under the sun,
a dead day in the Dead Sea of dead days
starting to turn a little smelly in the heat,

as one that has avoided ruin
and that promises something I will always try to understand
and will always—gladly—never understand,

and I keep coming back to it
as if it were the key to something,
and let the memory chip away at the present
like the sun chipped away at my flesh
as I stood under it, sweating, glad to be aging.

Hey man, you and I could be there too—
just bumming around,
trying out new versions of the old camaraderie.

THIRD WEEK IN MARCH

Monday, on the walk home,
the sun is still above the tree line
at 7:45 in the evening.
The pretzel-rod clouds are ribboned paths.

Tuesday, rain.
Wednesday, rain. Harder.

And then Thursday.
At 7:30 sharp,
the bare black trees
like shimmering silent murmurs,

you turn into the clearing
and lose yourself in a
rapturous lunar-blue sky.

Its piercing shade
astonishes, educates, connects.
How blessed you feel
for the fortune of being outside

at this exact moment in time,
with the weekend almost in sight.

Above, space seems not elegiac
nor tragic, not ecstatic
not even meditative
and not quite somber, but somehow transparent,

and the deepening saturation of color
is not seen but felt:
the heart's measure of time,
the heart's condensation of age—

A lifetime in one night,
a generation in a dusk,
a civilization in seconds.

The color is one
your mind could never invent,
nor could an artist truly capture,
only suggest—

perhaps a rare glimpse
of the soul of the sky,
ancient and very young
all at once.

Friday, at after-work drinks,
yesterday still glows
in your mind and heart,
and in your mind and heart

you toast yesterday,
no one knowing but you.

MARGARET HASSE

DAY AFTER DAYLIGHT SAVINGS

The blue numbers said I forgot
to change the clocks, which set
routines on haywire.

Like a domestic goat staked
to its circle of earth,
I don't do well untethered.

Outside a disruptive wind
turns leaves up-side-down,
provokes the eaves to whine.

I have no hunger for early dinner,
become confused by the sound
of children who seem out

too late for a school night.
They've found an extra helping
of daylight to romp on new grass.

They can't contain themselves,
strip off jackets, scatter
like a rag of ponies.

How can I regret one fugitive hour?
Whatever time says, children's joy
insists on springing forward.

WHAT THE WINDOW WASHERS DID

They arrived in a truck at 8 a.m.,
introduced themselves as Dave and Mike,
said no, they brought their own supplies
and equipment, said yes, pay in advance.
They circled the house, removing storms,
tugging at last year's ivy that cast its spell
of thatch across the east windows.

I opened the door to Mike, watched
as he positioned water bucket and rags.
Through grimed glass latticed with cobwebs,
Dave appeared on the outdoors side.
As if starting a fight, each lifted
his Windex bottles at the same time
and seemed to squirt the other in the face.

The men, silent as mimes in a mirror
with big hands tracing one another,
rubbed the surfaces of all the panes
until the glass squeaked and disappeared.
The sun, free to fly in, flung
a rectangle of light onto the floor.

MARY KAY RUMMEL

FIRST CRICKET AFTER WINTER
The quieter you become the more you are able to hear.—Rumi

1
The rasp I've been missing all winter
stops me on the way to bed.
When my eyes close I dream a cricket calling
through the silence in every grief.

2
Suddenly night is no longer enemy of day, time expands
beyond lonely into wide fields, the scent of dry
grasses, burnt honey of chaparral at dusk, coyote's
renegade choir under jasmine stars.

3
Comb-and-teasel, cracked violin
gypsy fiddler on my porch.
He breaks off yet tremolos
through me like north wind
through fig leaves.
How did I lose that coming-alive-in-all-things?

4
Sunrise. No singing.
Mourning dove's grey breast against grey wood.
She contemplates light among branches.
I remember cricket's scrape last night against the sky.
Dove blinks her liquid eye and I'm smitten with silence.

5
Until heavy steps of my neighbor in the hallway
and the low guttural rant of a television
across the courtyard shatters it.
I turn on Itzhak Perlman playing Klezmer,
scratch onto paper: *first cricket after winter.*
I don't know if any word can warm
an empty room or break a silence the way
this music burns and sweetens.

LAURENCE SNYDAL

A SUMMER DAY

It seems to me I always had enough
To do. Get up, eat shredded wheat and out
The door, grab my blue bike and ride about
A block to Jerry's house, undo my cuff
From the greasy bike chain, head to the zoo.
Look at the hawk who had no room to fly,
The den where a badger was said to lie,
And the frogs and the fish and turtles too
In their dank tank. Behind the flower shop
Deepen the hole in the vacant lot, find
Empty beer bottles someone left behind
And cash them in to buy an ice-cold pop.
Then eat lunch and a baseball game beset
With the kind of arguing you get when
You only have five players. It was then
That the summer sun reached zenith. So wet
With sweat we biked to the swimming pool, dove
Deep into water warmed by August heat
And when the grown-ups came at four, we beat
It, went back home to chores. The kitchen stove
Was cold. Sandwiches and milk that hot day.
Then in the long-drawn evening, kick-the-can
And bikes again and finally the fan
In the bedroom stirring still air away,
Sheer sheets shrouding a drowsy boy, at last
At rest and sleeping deeply in my past.

VI. COMMUNITY

ZACK ROGOW

SUNDAY MORNING BERNAL HEIGHTS
for Francine Slack, my freshman-year high school English teacher

Walking down from the crest of the hill
I glimpse the bay
fitting itself
snugly around the city.
A big black lab off-leash
bounds up
and shlurps my fingers.
"Maui," shouts the man behind him,
"stop that!" with a hint in his voice
that he knows there's no way
his dog will ever stop.
I buy bagels at the Good Life Grocery—
pumpernickel, onion,
everything. And lucky day!—
at the little latte shop I score
the last chocolate croissant for my daughter
with its tongue of dark flavor.
I pass a couple on the bench
in front of the Liberty Café,
the man weaving his arms together
to basket his baby
with its black lawn of hair,
an infant so new
the tags are just off,
and at that instant I know
I'm here to learn how to cherish
all that will endure
long after I'm gone
and even what has not yet
passed through the membrane.

A LITTLE BEFORE 3 P.M.

Barry and I walk down to the East River Bank
because he needs to cash a paycheck
and I need to withdraw a few dollars.
We jaywalk Amsterdam at 96th
and Barry points out the marble of Mary
outside the Church of the Holy Name.
The statue has bare feet
poking out from the bottom of her robes.
Barry goes to look for a post office
and I head toward Sunflowers,
which has the best buy in the neighborhood
on my favorite health food junk food.
The February sunlight plates everything on Broadway
with slightly tarnished silver.
The wind chaps my face.
Around 92nd Street I end up
behind an aging bum
who's ambling downtown.
In a guttural voice
he suddenly bursts into song:
This magic moment...

JOE COTTONWOOD

A GIFT OF BEACHES IN A BAG

At the bodega I bring a tub of sour cream
along with three one-dollar bills to Christine the cashier.
There's a sign taped to the counter:
　　FOUND!! In a Safeway bag!
　　"Memo Park" needs help
　　delivering a gift to Grandpa!!
Weird, and it's nine weeks since Christmas,
but recently I left some bags at the bodega
for customers to re-use. I never received a gift
from my grandson's family though they swear
they brought me one, so I say
"Hey. I think I might be that grandpa."

Sure enough, here's a gift wrapped with cartoons
on which a child scrawled in giant letters
　　TO GRANDPA
and then in smaller letters
　　from memo park.
My grandson lives near Menlo Park.
Age four, he's just learning to write.

So I open the gift wrapping.
Inside, a California State Parks Pass
good for an entire year of free entry.
It's a year's pass for walks on the beach!
My son knows I'm too cheap to go there
if I have to pay the park fee.

Thank you thank you so much
whoever opened the old sack,
whoever passed to me the gift of beaches in a bag.
The whole store is smiling. Christine forgets
to take my money until I remind her.
She hands me a penny in change, winks,
and says "Recycle. Shop local.
Good things will happen."

DAFFODIL MADMAN

From my bed I'd see the old nut
sneak out after midnight, pockets stuffed.
Before dawn he'd return, pockets empty.
In black of night he buried bulbs
in junk-strewn yards of Scuffletown,
paper-coated teardrops
lurking dormant under earth
while footprints faded.

My mother disapproved, afraid he'd get shot
and we couldn't waste money but
he never got caught.
A short man with spectacles, brown mustache,
schizoid, unemployed.
Me, a kid, to be seen with him was
murder by mortification.

Fifty years later and far away
they tell me all around Scuffletown
come bursts of yellow each April
from joy banked in dark times.

JAN SARCHIO

I DON'T GET IT

Chris has holes in his jacket, two of them, on the collar, at the back of his neckline. Fiberfill, the stuff they pack into pillows, is fingering its way out like a tiny polyester cloud. He doesn't care one lick about this course of events. He knows the holes are there, but the rest of the jacket, as far as I can see, is intact. Nan, one of his current "helpers" points to a picture of him that he has tacked to one of several bulletin boards in his room. He's on a motorcycle and he's wearing the same jacket. I tabulate the years between that photo and now and it's no less than twenty. This is the only jacket he's worn over that time, despite the fact that there are three "new" ones collecting dust in his closet.

We all try to take care of Chris. We all want to make sure he's warm, has pants without holes in the crotch, shirts that aren't frayed, socks that corral his wayward toes, hats that keep the snow or sun off, swimsuits that don't expose his privates, underwear with upstanding elastic, shoes with soles. You get my drift. So, with us (his mom and dad), friends, a sister, aunts and uncles all making sure that he's "covered," his closet is loaded.

He wears through things at a glacial rate. Even when there are obvious bits missing, he is content to continue wearing them. "It's still good," he tells me about his trusty jacket, while I wave a new one in front of him, as if I am a matador and he is Ferdinand. He has nothing against the new things, but he is attached to the old. It's as if they are part of him, like old buddies. He holds on until the last thread snaps. He does this with blankets, sheets, upholstered furniture, well, he does it with everything. He still has some music tapes. He howls with great emotional pain when they get irreparably tangled in his tape player. In order to part with them he unreels all of the tape, cuts it into confetti, puts it in the trash, and weeps. We get him replacement CD's, which helps, but the old items seem to be woven into the fabric of him. When blankets, shirts, appliances, etc. break, he has to finish the job, rending them into tiny bits and casting them away. His twenty-year-old jacket has a long way to go.

I remember when he rode that motorcycle in the photo. He still lived with us and once a week we had a "helper" come and take him out and do "guy" stuff. I remember when Dwayne drove up our long driveway on his bike. He knocked at the door, holding an extra helmet and my heart fell to my feet. He was decked out in leathers, covered in tats, beard, headband and a smile as big as the sky. He saw the concern on my face, but somehow managed to get me to say "okay" to Chris riding with him on the back of his hog.

"You have to wear a helmet and hold on tight, Buddy," he said to Chris.

"Yeah?" Chris replied. He was not one to be confined and a helmet was a true novelty for him. But the carrot, a ride over hill and dale and a visit to Home Depot, was worth it. "Okay," he nodded.

"I'll take good care of him," Dwayne said.

And they were off.

I've often thought of that big, burly, teddy bear man driving through town with a twenty-four-year-old autistic dude holding tight to his chest. So much of life I don't understand. Cruelty, snow, how cats purr, what causes pain, the attachment to old jackets, and miraculous kindness. Maybe life isn't about understanding; maybe it's about enjoying the ride. Vrooooom.

ANDREW PAUL GRELL

A CHRISTMAS BREAK MIRACLE

Funny thing about numbers, when they start getting associated with people. Some people want a better one of whichever type of number they're associated with: weight, IQ, salary, adept level, apartment building floor, pinball score. Even if the numbers don't get you very much. An extra ball or a free game at pinball. The knowledge that an admin on some internet group certifies that you are more hip to the tenets of the group than other people. Or, in my case, about $3.50.

A company named Alta operates CitibikeNYC, the official bike sharing service in New York and Hoboken. For $150 a year, you can take care of almost all of your in-city traveling. Even if you don't bike all that regularly, just having an annual key gives you an option of not spending another twenty bucks on a cab ride, or, if that cab is stuck in traffic, a way to make a curtain time for your $200 tickets. Or to avoid *getting* $200 parking tickets! The share system may be the pinnacle of economic efficiency. It's like the public library. You can drop by and see what's available, or log in and download, or put yourself on a reserve list and the book will show up at your branch and they'll email you. The cost of reading, in this case, funded by original endowments, local taxes, and current donors, goes way down while ensuring authors at least a minimum level of sales. In the case of Bike Share, the municipality grants rights of way for the stations, regular users pay their dues, tourists pay proportionally more for short-term memberships. The city gets a new transportation platform at no capital cost, and a reduction in cars being driven in, potentially lowering lung disease cases and asthma attacks. The share system software tries to make sure that bikes (and open spaces to return bikes) are available as needed. But that doesn't always work.

Cycling is, as well as being a different mode of transportation, a different way of seeing and being. A woman on Manhattan's east side made a painting career of capturing the same Central Park tree, in every season, year after year. Someone driving uptown on the Park Drive wouldn't notice anything, but the cyclists and runners did. You could stop and admire the work, see it change day to day, have a conversation with an artist. A mystery sculptor all the way across town, on the Hudson River paths in Riverside Park, would assemble driftwood into assorted shapes. Only by transiting the work slowly could the intended representation pop out, a rabbit, for example, or a Santa Claus, becoming art from piles of sticks. One day a party of Japanese tourists visited that stretch of the park, and left a rock-tower sculpture behind, in harmony with the driftwood. Cars, sometimes only yards east, are shut out of this gallery.

My own cycling has become more mundane, of late, than this grand vision. With three arthritises, and a fourth bubbling up my spine, the only way I can reasonably get around Manhattan is by bike. I still have the fire in my belly of cycling to reduce lung disease, the effects of global warming, and resource wars, but the hundred-mile trip days are long over. Although I'm still riding enough to keep in shape.

It takes a lot for me to get excited about scores and points and other numbers being associated with me. Duane Reade has an easy rewards point system, when you check out, they know who you are and give you your reward, so I shop there; CVS's program requires you to keep miles of receipts. Speaking of miles, Marlboro miles started out well. Our upstate friends Harry and Wendy would "volunteer" to help sweep up at their local bar at closing time. They swept up enough first-generation miles to get a little fold-up towable camper. I still have some of the Marlboro stuff; a knapsack I still use to this day, and the best jeans jacket I ever had, from my second-generation miles. But as the program rolled on, the value-per-mile ratio started slipping until it was barely worth the effort. But just a few months ago, while deep in a multi-dimensional funk about work (including the untimely death of a colleague and friend, whose workload I had to pick up), our dog's health, and squaring away my Dad's nursing home, and we were moving our offices, and somehow, I found that I was responsible for things I had no idea about how they worked. I was invited to be an Angel, and get Angel Points. I could have used an angel myself!

When the library flaunts its efficiencies, it moves books around in vans, from where a book lives to the branch where someone wants it, and from where another reader returns it to its home branch. My branch is Tompkins Square, where Yip Harburg wrote the songs for *The Wizard of Oz*. When

Citibike balances the stations, it's a little more complicated. Bikes can be loaded into trucks and vans, and that works for balancing stations north and south of each other, but not east-west. You simply can't travel cross-town in Manhattan at anything faster than walking pace. Some solutions were to have "bicycle-pulled trailers" moving eight bikes at a time; or to have "valet stations" with room to stock extra bikes. These were only partly successful. Hence, the creation of the Bike Angel.

The concept is simple. If an Angel takes a bike out from a station that has a lot of bikes, and then returns it to a station with very few bikes, the Angel is awarded points based on an algorithm. Some folks live near a station which is chronically full and work near a station that is consistently under-biked. These people have it made. Then some people can go an extra few, sometimes more than a few to find an overloaded station and at their terminus, be willing to walk a bit more to put their bike in a needy spot. The latter is how I started out; Alta was offering a five-times-points special on docking bikes north of 59th Street. It would be an extra three hundred yards for me. I racked up some points that way, but I was going over my "available steps" budget for the day, and one of my "iteses," Plantar Fasciitis, kicked in. But I stayed in the program, and from time to time a random trip would garner me a point or two. And then I found out that if you got twenty points in a month, you got a free one-week extension of your membership! A target! A goal!

The holiday break came, and I was blissfully off work. I love solving problems more than any old point system. How could I take a few hours moving bikes around without using up my available "steps" getting to eligible stations? While not a traffic engineer, and not really a systems analyst, although I play one in my office, I was associated with some very fine examples of both of those categories. It was time to put what I knew from talking with these people into good use. And of course, the answer was the general solution for making transportation efficient anywhere: Multi-Mode Transportation. Park & Ride, commuter rail to local subway, bus-ferry-bus, busses with bike racks.

Commuting could be a quadrathlon. In fact, in my old long-distance cycling days, I used to bike up to the George Washington Bridge and across and down to Edgewater to shop in the Japanese shopping center, Mitsuwa. And then back. I thought that was pretty cool. And then one day I saw two guys in a kayak—the fourth leg of the quadrathlon—coming from the Manhattan side and beaching on the riverbank at the rear of the mall. No matter how cool you think you are, there is always someone cooler than thou.

I thought commuting to work by bike was cool in the 90s, until I started seeing a guy commuting (suit, briefcase) by unicycle on Broadway's new bike lane.

So it was that one morning on the break, I took down my old Xootr kick-scooter, and kicked it over to my local bike docking station to see if I could rig it to be carried in the bike's front-carrier. Bingo! I rode the scooter to the nearest over-filled station, secured the scooter, and rode to the nearest empty station. Then rode the scooter back. And back again. And again. I calculated that scooter rides used about one-third the "step budget" as walking. When the stations approached symmetry, losing their point values, possibly because other folks capable of walking between stations were doing what I was doing for points, I moved it over to a dicier part of town, Alphabet city. Those stations were almost always overloaded. The bikeshare software sends a message whenever an Angel earns points, accompanied by cheerful alert sound, with an inspiring message about how a more earthly rider was helped by the actions of the Angel. And sometime around 11:45, I got the email I wanted: I had earned a free week, but still got to keep my points for goodies like giving day-passes to friends. Joy! Triumph! Ecstasy!

I had always though of cyclists as knights errant. We are armored (those of us who wear helmets, that is.) We are mounted. We are quick to assist each other, or anyone, when needed. Did you ever see a car stop to clear a hazard—stray garbage can, peeled tire – from a street? We are the Knights of Velocia. But now, I know that I am an Angel.

We made the move, with the standard number of screw-ups, all handled. A fee of $4,500 to a law firm in Florida, for the services of their benefits paralegal (who happened to be the mother of our favorite baseball player) who straightened out my Dad's benefits. The dog is tolerating and responding to treatment; I can hope she will ride with me again when it gets a little warmer, and maybe I can run our neighbor's dog on the scooter, too. And I'm an Angel!

Post Scriptum
Our dog "went over the rainbow bridge" a month after I wrote this memoir-ette. It was the first time I ever cried at losing a loved one; I could have cried my own River Styx. Our marriage hit its nadir while arguing about when or whether to get a new dog. We then discovered that a nadir is not the lowest point,

but rather has a bargain basement, just like Macy's and Gimbels used to have: an early effort to get another Rat Terrier turned into a horrifying episode of peri-anaphylactic shock allergic episodes.

My Dad followed Nora two months later. He went into hospice care, went to sleep one night and didn't wake up the next morning.

We now have a new hypo-allergenic puppy, fourteen weeks old. He has klutzy puppy legs and wants to be friends with everyone. Each time I walk him, I am vicariously surprised by the joy that surprises Cyrus.

ROSEMARY VOLZ

CHRISTINE

Christine is sitting at the kitchen table.
It is four a.m. and she can't sleep.
She is reading the Psalms.
And though she is not religious, she has
Sunday clothes and a schoolyard fear of God.
Christine is as ordinary as a sunset,
As spectacular as a loaf of bread.
She is wearing an old but lovely sweater—
The third button is missing.
She likes the 56th Psalm which tells us
God puts our tears in a bottle.
She imagines a room filled with glass bottles.
The bottles are resting on wooden shelves
And each bottle has a brass plate with a name engraved on it.
How intimate this sounds; no tears are hidden from the almighty.
The good Lord knows all about our unremarkable hearts.
Christine thinks that there must be more female names than male
Because she has rarely seen men cry.
Even her lovers saved their tears for someone else.
Perhaps men don't cry but weep and sob.
Yes, she remembers her father sobbing when
She told him she was having an abortion.
She didn't have it and Michael turned out to be
The grandson who gave the eulogy at his funeral.
And Michael wept.
And even though her parents were at war for many years,
Her mother cried without shame when her father died.
Just thinking of all those tears makes Christine cry.
She blows her nose and then it comes to her—

There is a human sameness to sorrow.
There are no separate bottles;
There is just one big bottle and the collective tears of the wounded are in it.
The story about that the moon controlling the tides is just a myth.
The pouring out of that bottle is what makes the ocean rise.
The pouring out of that bottle is what makes the seas salty.
Christine is so proud of her enlightenment that
She pours out some corn flakes, closes the Bible and yawns.

MARGARET DeRITTER

TABLES OF STRANGERS AT THE CHINESE BUFFET

Four Amish boys can't keep their eyes off
our lengthy table of lesbians, keep turning
around in their bowl cuts and blue shirts,
away from their mother and sister in dresses
and bonnets, to marvel at these unlikely
creatures who are having so much fun.

What do the brothers make of our short
haircuts and raucous laughter? The boyish
faces looking back at them? Do they notice
all the pants, the random nose rings? A woman's
hand on another's hair? Why so many women,
they must wonder, with no men around?

I can almost hear their neurons racing,
feel a tug from their searching eyes.
Are we a sewing circle? A bowling league?
Their faces are friendly, inquisitive, yearning.
Yes, I want to say, it's okay to have questions.
It's okay to come over and chat.

We're curious about you too. Do you like to wear
those black suspenders? Do you imagine yourself
in some Nike Airs? Do you wish your sister could
let down her hair? Do you long to run off to Chicago
or grow the world's tastiest corn? Oh, sweet boys,
the world is filled with unspoken desires.

Think about a bumblebee landing on an obedient
plant, diving into an open flower, unfurling
her tongue when she senses the nectar. Reach out
for your dreams like that. Suck all the sweetness
you can from this life. Chase what you want.
Love whom you will. Trample the rules.

The world won't always love you, but this day
it does. When you serve us your smiles,
we send ours right back. And when your daddy
walks by at the end of the night with your sister
held tight in his arms, even he smiles too—
so hard to resist all the joy in this room.

LOWELL JAEGER

THE BUBBLES

Jet-lagged, we snugged the covers over our ears
to muffle *las campañas de la catedral*, tolling.
Stepped into the midday sun, blinded by how far
the day had progressed without us. Hungry
enough to settle for a vendor's cart menu,
plastic tables and worn umbrellas, across from the plaza
where someone had switched on
fountains of spray hissing skyward and falling,
sizzling on the hot streets like rain.

Not a fountain, really, but jets
or nozzles embedded in the cobbles and brickwork,
firing at random for the simple screams
of barefoot niños dashing to soak
their camisetas y pantelones for the joy of what
dazzle might rise on a Sunday afternoon.
And did I mention the children blowing bubbles?

Not blowing them, really, but throwing them
from homemade coat-hanger wands dipped
in pails of sudsy dish soap. Huge soap balloons
taking shape as the children twirled and laughed.
Families cheering the bubbles as each rose toward the sun,

undulating liquid rainbows. Kaleidoscopic rainbows!
As my wife and I held hands across the table,
glad to be in love amidst the bustle,
this world's wondrous and baffling extravagance,
thousands of miles from home.

KELLY TALBOT

THE FIRST AMERICAN

Standing on the edge of the Black Sea,
I watch as the copper pre-dawn waves
roll endlessly toward my bare feet
as if they are desperate to reach me,
as if I have weight, gravity,
as if I am the moon pulling at them
while reflecting the sun's power,
as if I could save them if only
they could reach me. I am but a man,
not the moon. I cannot save the waves.

I know that beyond the horizon
war machines of my countrymen
rain fire and death down on the homes
of men, their engines roaring "freedom"
across the land to end terror,
never uttering the word "empire,"
and there is nothing that I can do.

Saddened, I turn back toward the beach
and see the small Turkish boy who sells
baklavah sitting, taking a break.
I walk over and ask him if he plays
backgammon. His eyes light up and
soon we are playing game after game.
To keep him out of trouble, I buy
his pastries as we play, and we speak
of seagulls, our sandals, this season's
tangerines. We tell each other our names.

Then, my new friend asks me
"Where are you from?" "America."
I am his first American. He laughs and says
"You are white, like the moon."
I feel myself pulling gently
at the boy, the waves, and the world.
Maybe I am not a man.
Maybe I am the moon.

TERRI ELDERS

DIFFERENT BUT DIVINE

In Jewish history there are no coincidences. " – Elie Wiesel

"I don't expect you to become Jewish," Frank said. "I'm only asking you to stay your own curious and open-minded self and come to a synagogue with me for Sabbath."

My mouth dropped open. "But they'll be speaking Hebrew," I sputtered. "I don't know a word of that language. I won't have any idea what's going on."

He laughed and patted my hand. "It's easy. It's a Reform temple, so the sermon will be in English. Do what everybody else does. If I stand up, you stand up. When somebody says something to you, repeat what they say back to them. Works every time."

Easy for him to say. After all, my new boyfriend was a retired university professor who'd taught the history of Judaism. "Four thousand years in fourteen weeks," he'd quipped of his introductory course.

Though I harbored serious doubts, I agreed to go. During my childhood in rural Oregon, I'd won a New Testament for faithful Sunday School attendance at a tiny Friends Church. The Quaker philosophy stuck with me. I've always relied on my "Inner Light" to help me distinguish between good and evil, and to reassure me of the infinite love of God.

In adulthood, my church-going mainly has been limited to weddings and funerals. As a Peace Corps Volunteer, I'd dropped in on a few services here and there: A Harvest Festival at the "Scots" St. Andrew's Presbyterian Church in Belize City; a nondenominational Easter observance at the Episcopal Cathedral in Santo Domingo; even a Christmas Eve candlelight ceremony at Immaculate Conception in Victoria, Seychelles.

But a Jewish Sabbath? When I looked up what women were expected to wear at a Reform Shabbat, I discovered I'd even been misspelling "synagogue." How would I manage to not embarrass myself, let alone Frank, who so graciously had invited me?

On Friday evening, I tightly gripped his hand as we entered the foyer. Even though he'd donned his yarmulke and prayer shawl, he still looked just like the friendly gentleman that I'd begun to fall in love with, extraordinary for the two of us, both nearing eighty. I believed I could trust him to guide me throughout the evening. Nothing would go wrong.

Until it did. I soon discovered I'd no idea what people were murmuring as they twined arms behind one another's backs and swayed. I tried in vain to make out their words. I realized I had more homework to do.

Frank previously had told me that the "siddur," the prayer book, would have a Hebrew text, followed by the Hebrew text transliteration into my own familiar alphabet, and then a translation into English, so I could follow along with the rabbi or cantor. At the bottom of each page I discovered fascinating explanatory notes. Some referenced passages from historic and modern poets and philosophers that I'd long revered.

I'd learned that Hebrew is read from right to left and knew to open the book from the right-hand side. But then I committed a major error. Once again people began to link hands. We were crowded together, so without thinking I set the book down...on the floor. I heard the woman next to me gasp and saw Frank's eyes widen.

"Pick it up and kiss it," he whispered. "It's sacred. Never put it on the floor." I bent down, grabbed it, hurriedly kissed it, and placed it on the rack in front of me. It was all I could do to fight back the tears that threatened to flood down my scarlet cheeks.

As he drove me home that evening, Frank attempted to reassure me. He had founded an interfaith network and attended all kinds of ceremonies associated with religions I'd only vaguely heard of.

"I have many Muslim friends," he said, "so during Ramadan I get invited a lot of Iftar feasts. That's when they break their fast after sunset. The first time I went I expected that the food would be like Mediterranean. I'd known there'd be Indian dishes, and I'd thought of Indian Muslims as quiet, reflective, nonaggressive. But the food wasn't passive at all. It was all curries and hot spices and it grabbed my throat and I coughed and choked and people stared."

He continued to try to comfort me. "At the Sikh Gurdwara the first time I went, I was glad somebody had taken the time to explain to me not to point my feet toward the platform that displayed their holy book."

I began to feel better. I'd experienced something similar when I did some training for Peace Corps in Mongolia, where pointing feet toward divine objects also is considered taboo.

It's taken me a lot more than the fourteen weeks of Frank's course to learn about his religion. Nevertheless, I've continued to progress, and Frank remains an ever-patient teacher. The second time I accompanied him to a synagogue, I knew to say, "Shabbat shalom," which means "Sabbath of peace." I didn't make any horrendous gaffes. By Rosh Hashanah, the beginning of the Jewish calendar year, I could say "L'shana tova," Hebrew for "a good year." In December as Chanukah neared, I carefully wrapped the traditional eight small gifts for my beloved, one for each day of the observance.

Recently Frank and I visited London during the time of Purim, and we attended the jolly celebration of the events related in the book of Esther at a synagogue there. I loved watching the children in their storybook costumes as they booed at the name of the villain, Haman, and cheered at the name of the heroine, Esther. I savored the buttery little three-cornered Hamantachen tarts.

As Passover approached, Frank, still respecting that I wasn't becoming Jewish, felt comfortable enough to schlep me to more religious functions. In addition to his doctorate in sociology, my boyfriend also holds a Doctor of Divinity degree, and is an ordained Reform rabbi. Invited to conduct Passover services aboard the Queen Elizabeth on its leg between Victoria, Seychelles, where I used to be a Peace Corps Volunteer, and Cape Town, South Africa, Frank asked me to accompany him.

I'd long dreamed of returning to this Indian Ocean paradise where I'd worked for three years as a Peace Corps Volunteer. I remembered once sitting on a high granitic peak there, watching the QE2, the predecessor of the current Cunard liner, sail into port.

Never had I ever guessed I'd return decades later, to sail out from that sparkling harbor on a cruise myself, accompanied by the clergyman who would be conducting Seder.

At Seder, he asked if anybody present wasn't Jewish. Four people raised their hands. Sheepishly, so did I. I could see astonished faces on some who seemed surprised that the Rabbi's partner wasn't Jewish. Frank winked at me as I blushed, before sampling my gefilte fish.

Frank reminds me that in his faith, there's no room for chance or coincidence. That we met and fell in love at our ages is Divine Providence.

I still find the basic message I learned in childhood at the Friends Church is shared by his Jewish beliefs . . . that human worth is measured in acts of loving kindness, doing justice, valuing mercy, and walking humbly with God.

VII. RESILIENCE/ILLNESS

ANDREA HANSELL

THE FLOWERS AND BUBBLES OF JOY

Four months after my husband died I experienced joy again. Before that moment I had alternated between raw grief and a numb, detached state. I would sit at my kitchen table with a cup of morning coffee, thinking nothing, feeling nothing, and then find that it was afternoon, the coffee was cold, and I still hadn't showered or dressed. At unpredictable intervals a reminder of the finality of my husband's death, such as the layer of dust building up on his unplayed guitar, would set a blow torch to my frozen emotions. Then I would cry, sometimes for hours.

But one August afternoon I sat down in a lawn chair on my patio and opened a novel I'd looked forward to reading. Birds chirped and fluttered around the bird feeder, and the scent of sun-warmed roses wafted over from a neighbor's yard. I bit into a peach I had just bought at the local farmers' market and experienced a rush of peachness—not the mealy, faintly sweet taste of winter supermarket peaches, but the spiced velvet essence of ripe, just-picked fruit. I licked the peach juice from my lips and realized that I was feeling joy. I knew then that I would live, and not just live but thrive. The plotline of the rest of my life would not be the smoothly happy one I had expected, but joy would still be part of the story.

The surfacing of joy after a deep, dark period of grief led me to think back over my years of psychotherapy work with depressed and traumatized clients. Some of my clients seemed to have been born resilient, with a positive life force that could be suppressed by bad experiences but not eradicated. These individuals were able to cling to tiny rafts of positive experiences in the cold sea of trauma, and after the trauma was over, they could make their way back to the warmth of dry land.

Early in my training I interviewed a survivor of the Nazi concentration camps. She told me of an afternoon when she and another girl in a children's camp were able to reach through a wire fence and grab some weedy yellow flowers they saw growing on the other side. The girls sat in the barren dust on their side of the fence and wove the flowers into golden crowns and necklaces for each other. It was, the woman recalled, a moment of pure joy in the midst of overwhelming loss and terror. In her adult life, though dogged by post-traumatic stress symptoms and grief for family members who had perished, she was able to find joy in music, in sunsets, and in the flowers of her own garden.

Later in my career I encountered a number of clients who were unable to feel any joy at all, sometimes for long periods of time. This inability to experience pleasure, technically termed anhedonia, is one of the diagnostic criteria of a major depressive episode. I recall a client with a traumatic childhood history and treatment-resistant depression who told me she had tried hobby after hobby in an effort to feel positively invested in something, anything. But she was not able to sustain her interest. She left the new vegetable garden half-planted and weedy, and knit only one sleeve of a sweater. She felt so bored, so empty, that she felt she was just waiting for death. She wasn't actively suicidal, she assured me; it was just that if someone told her she'd die in a car accident tomorrow she wouldn't care. But wouldn't there be anything she'd miss, I asked her, her cat, a summer day, music, something that brought her joy? "No," she said. "I know that's not what you want to hear, but no."

I wondered then, as I wonder now, what gives some of us the ability to more easily find life's yellow flowers, its glorious ripe peaches? As a therapist, could I help lead a patient to joy? I wasn't sure that I could spark joy in someone who had never felt it. But if a person, through some combination of genetics and environmental stress, had temporarily lost the ability to feel pleasure, I could assure them that if they once felt joy, they would feel it again. Then I could help them identify and nurture any small, quiet stirrings of pleasure that began to resurface.

I worked with a young woman who became deeply depressed after the suicide of a much-loved younger sister. Formerly cheerful and enthusiastic, my client now plodded joylessly through life. Then one evening she idly turned on the Summer Olympics on TV. She began to watch the gymnastics competitions, recalling that she and her sister had taken gymnastics together as children. She learned the names of the American gymnasts, some facts about their lives. She found discussion boards online where fans discussed the competition, the scoring, the post-Olympics futures of the gymnasts. When she met with me on the day of the individual event finals, I observed to her that she seemed to be looking forward to watching the competition that night, that she might even enjoy it. "Oh, no," she said immediately. "It's dumb."

A moment later she smiled. "You know," she said, "I think I might be enjoying the gymnastics a little."

The realization showed her both that she could still treasure shared positive memories involving her sister, and that she had not irrevocably lost her capacity for pleasure. It was an early step in a recovery that eventually brought joy to my client, and to me as her therapist as well.

Last week I had lunch with my 103-year-old cousin, an admirable woman who is still a working artist with her own studio. When we left the restaurant she said it had been nice talking with me, but she couldn't wait to get back to her kitchen.

"What's in your kitchen?" I asked.

She told me that she had recently begun studying digital photography. That morning she had set a baking tray in her kitchen sink at a slant and had poured soapy water down it, introducing various obstacles to block and change the flow of the bubbles. Then she had photographed the bubbles. "I'm so enjoying it!" she said.

I wish I could attribute my cousin's long life to her capacity for joy, but I have known too many people, including my own husband, who died too early despite taking great joy in the world around them. What I can say, though, is that if one is going to live to 103, it would be a blessing to have those years be full of yellow flower crowns, of sweet, ripe peaches, and of shiny bubbles that divide around obstacles and re-form to flow onwards.

ZAN BOCKES

ASK ME AGAIN TOMORROW:
MOOD SWINGS ON THE BIPOLAR PENDULUM

For many years, I could not anticipate my state of mind from one day to the next. Making plans a week ahead of time proved impossible. Perhaps I would be suicidal or bedridden or afraid to leave the house. Or I'd be in the middle of a bout of mania, so disorganized I couldn't communicate and so full of energy I couldn't sit still. I might be plagued with hallucinations—shadowy figures advancing in the periphery of my vision and androgynous voices in my head berating me and ordering me around. Dealing with these symptoms was a daily chore, and their severity varied unpredictably. A question asked one day could receive a completely opposite answer the next.

During most of my adult life, instability defined the norm—I knew of no other way to be. I marveled at friends who scheduled things ahead of time and carried out their duties with little difficulty. I felt inferior to these people and angry at myself for not being more responsible.

Not even the diagnosis of severe bipolar disorder seemed a good excuse, as I didn't think it applied to me. As a writer, I only suffered from the usual writerly ailments of acute perspicuity and deep despair. I thought, to quote Rainer Maria Rilke, "Don't take my devils away or my angels may flee." Creativity had its price, and I was willing to pay.

The friends and relatives around me, however, disapproved of this exchange, especially when I depended on their involvement to save me from my erratic self. They thought I needed help; I thought I was just being me.

Unsurprisingly, I spent an inordinate amount of time in psychiatric hospitals. The doctors reined me in with powerful pharmaceuticals, seclusion and restraints. I rarely complied with the prescribed treatments, as I hated the medications and their side effects—weight gain, sedation, drooling, restlessness, urinary incontinence, constipation, blurred vision and an overall sense of deadness and zombie-ism. Almost all of these drugs reduced my creativity and took away the emotional extremes I'd valued. I couldn't read or write or think—my curiosity and energy vanished.

But the auditory hallucinations disappeared too—a big relief. No longer did they command me to do everything from "Sit up straight!" to "Off yourself!" The niggling conversations and accusatory remarks diminished to the quiet hum of purposeful thought and casual observations—the intended purpose of the drugs. But I did not like the tradeoff. I wavered between stifling sedation and a screaming pinnacle of awareness, neither state bearable for very long.

On meds, I missed the intensity of that pinnacle—the state of being alive, alert, awake and aware. I missed the midnight revelations and powerful dreams (when I could sleep), and the zinging push to experience and embrace Life, grab it by the horns, climb on its back and ride. The doctors warned me against "dangerous hypomania," which angered me because it seemed they wouldn't permit me to feel good. They dangled the threat of disaster over my head like a dagger. But their words of caution rarely went unjustified.

Had I settled gradually to a more balanced state, being "out of control" would not have been an issue. Unfortunately for all involved, the mood usually did not remain there—it increased to a terrifying frenzy of disconnectedness, loud voices, a shattering of all familiar and the sensations of my skin turning to rubber and the top of my brain lifting off, exposed to cool air. The earth undulated beneath me. I stayed up for several nights in a row. Frequently I heard *the music of the spheres*, long bell notes pealing across the dark sky. Indecipherable messages unwound urgently across the ceiling in brilliant red sand. I strode the city streets, talking aloud to myself, knowing I looked scary and silly, but compelled to continue.

Sooner or later, my jubilance passed and I plunged into a dim, grey world where daylight disappeared. My tears and misery threatened to drown me. Suicide seemed the only option, and over the years I made several near-fatal attempts.

In 1995, two added words further refined my diagnosis of bipolar disorder: "Rapid cycling." I averaged five to six severe episodes and two to three hospitalizations a year, and sometimes my mood yanked from one extreme to another in a matter of hours.

One good example of this catapulting occurred during a hospital stay that was temporarily interrupted when I escaped from the locked ward.

Admitted with a diagnosis of psychotic depression, I lay in bed in a dark room for several days, the world so oppressively black that all I managed to do was stare at the crisscross pattern on my blanket. Trays of food came and went, untouched. My body had become a sodden corpse.

I have no idea what suddenly motivated me to leave the bed and step out into the small, locked courtyard where patients better off hung out and drank decaffeinated coffee. At this moment, everyone else was inside. I sat at the picnic table and looked blankly at the top of the roof, where the sharp blue sky met the peak high above me. My gaze fell to the garbage can below, and I mused briefly about this arrangement.

As though guided by a paranormal force, I climbed atop the garbage can, reached up to the gutter and pulled myself up. I am still amazed at my strength and agility after the long days in bed. When I stepped stealthily across the shingles, I looked briefly through the skylight at my fellow patients milling about the dayroom. I could jump through the glass and surely die. I could attract attention by dancing and waving to those below. But I had a better idea—crawl across the roof to the outside slope, jump fifteen feet down and run away. Which is what I did.

I shuffled along downtown Omaha's streets, my mind still slightly foggy, the noise of passing cars a distant roar as I strove to process where I was and what I'd done. Then I saw the shimmering summer sun descending over the horizon in liquid gold, filtering through the trees—a glorious splendor of light, touched with incredible sadness because of its ephemeral nature. Evening threatened total and terrifying darkness. The prospect of the day's loss brought tears to my eyes and a swelling of emotion in my chest. I entertained the notion of killing myself by leaping into traffic, but the gold coins of dappled sunset showed me the riches I possessed, encouraging me to stick around and find out what would happen next. I had escaped and survived the Hell of the hospital, able now to appreciate Beauty at its finest as it surrounded me, displaying its colors for me alone to see, a gift from the Powers of the Universe persuading me to live with a vengeance, let Life itself lift me on its shining wings.

I waltzed the five miles back to my apartment and phoned a friend, telling her that I was "Well! Discharged! Free! Given the Seal of Approval and Allowed to go Home!" To my surprise, she didn't trust all this ebullience and called the hospital. In the three hours since I'd escaped, the staff hadn't even noticed my absence. Because I was unwilling to return, the police appeared and took me back in handcuffs. My mood plummeted again, only lengthening my stay.

With all this tumult, it may be difficult to understand my reluctance to swallow the pills that steadied me. Being *steady* felt like an oppression of my spirit, a hunk of mud on my brain, and I equated *recovery* with being dead and emotionless, complacent and bored. The *cure,* I decided, was worse than the disease. But no one else saw it that way.

Eventually, after many psychiatric hospitalizations, I began to reconsider. I learned my highs exceeded "a good mood," and my depressions fell lower than "the blues" or ordinary sadness. The professionals kept emphasizing this until I began to accept that maybe they had a point—most people did not attempt suicide or stride boldly into traffic joyously singing. The potential harm alarmed my few remaining friends.

I owe much to these people. They patiently weathered my storms, offering guiding hands when I strayed too close to the cliff. They took me to the hospital when my condition became critical, and they came to visit me. All this, when I could not reciprocate the friendship in any meaningful way.

I am now fifty-eight years old. My troubles began at nineteen. Sometimes I feel the illness has stolen huge chunks of my life. I spent long periods unemployed and dropped out of college repeatedly. Nevertheless, I successfully completed a BA in English, and a BFA and MFA in Creative Writing, despite the prediction that I'd never be well enough to return to college. My first collection of poetry, *Caught in Passing,* was published in 2013.

Although I was told that my condition would only worsen with age, I've made an unprecedented recovery in the past several years. Improved medications help me use my other coping skills, with fewer side effects. My poetry and fiction continue to sustain me, and I find I can write and work more consistently without being swayed by my mood vicissitudes. It is easier to cultivate friendships and return their kindnesses, and to follow through with plans and obligations.

I still have episodes of illness, though nowhere near as severe or frequent, and I've learned enough about my warning symptoms to catch problems early. I've grown accustomed to being cheerful, productive, creative and reliable, enjoying a stability previously unknown to me. My only wish is to maintain my current quality of life, and if you ask me again tomorrow, my answer will be the same.

KELLY TALBOT

IMPACT

After the crash
words make no sense;
letters hold no meaning.
"This" twists into "isthmus,"
"memory" melts into "ember,"
"name" contorts into "enemy,"
and "confusion" shatters into "confusion."

Outside the window, the hyacinths
are beginning to bloom.
She daydreams of becoming
a gardener, but they keep
bringing her chocolates,
telling her that they know
she hates flowers. She doesn't
even know who they are.
They keep telling her
who she was, but her eyes
follow from shadow to light
the delicate curves of petals
as the hyacinths blossom.
How can she ever know
if what was really was,
if what is really is?
They keep telling her.

They don't know that one day soon
she will have moist soil
under her nails,
reaching for the sun
and finally flowering.

RUTH MARGOLIN SILIN

THEY CUT A HOLE

where none had been and
stitched me up like a shirt
in need of mending.
Beeps became a symphony &
angels in scrubs offered mini cups
of water to make pink pills
go down.
Curtains drawn open, body
parts probed, flesh and sex overrated
commodities, like utilities with
unpaid bills.

The house looked strange until
someone adjusted the shades &
let the light shine on the prayer plant,
leaves in supplicant position.
In the shower, hot soapy water flowed over
the scar, a few tiny bubbles reluctant to leave
& the scent of antiseptic overpowered by
Este Lauder's lotion.
I inhaled like a nomad coming upon
a stream, grabbed a towel & shouted
   "Yes, Yes, Yes!"

JENNIFER L. FREED

RESULTS

Benign!
And you rise on the news
with yellow wings,
a tulip song.

Benign!
So easy, now, to stay aloft.
Even today's gray clouds
an invitation.

How delicious,
the neighbor's ever-barking dog,
the incessant call
of dirty dishes, laundry, dust.

Soon enough they'll lose their gloss.
You know this.
But for now—benign!—you float,
feeling blessed by the mundane.

WEIHUA ZHANG

MAKING A SNOWMAN

Having lived in Savannah, Georgia, for almost twenty-two years, snow is the rarest scene to behold. I can't recall any sizable snow accumulations all those years since I moved to Savannah in August 1996 to accept a teaching job at The Savannah College of Art and Design. Hence, Winter Storm Grayson 2018 came as a welcoming surprise. When the white fluffy snow miraculously fell from the sky on an unusual wintry day, it took my mind off my scary recent diagnosis. I never thought that this once-in-almost-thirty-year weather phenomenon could bring a much-needed relief to my heartache, sadness, and angst. For the first time in two weeks, I found myself laughing into oblivion, as if there were no tomorrow.

January 3, 2018 started with a freezing rain, with the high temperature dipping below the twenties. Historically, the average high for Savannah in January is in the sixties, so this was quite a drop. By noontime the freezing rain had turned into flurry, which quickly intensified. Fat snowflakes kept piling up, leaving a thick blanket of snow on our driveway and the front lawn. A rare winter wonderland. You have to understand that *thick* is by Savannah standard—where a trace of snow coupled with freezing temperature could cause havoc on the road. The sudden drop in temperature proved too much for our twelve-year old heating unit, which struggled mightily to crank up to sixty-six degrees. Bundled up with layers of clothes, I watched the snow from our dining room window, my aching heart growing heavier by the minute. I was not in the mood to enjoy the snow, however rare it might have been. In anticipation of the frozen roadways and snow, many schools, businesses, clinics and hospitals had closed for the day. Among them, The Center for Digestive & Liver Health, my doctor's office. I'd just had a CT scan the day prior and was anxious to get the result and possible treatment options. Now the snow had put everything on hold.

After an extremely busy fall quarter ended on Nov. 14, 2017, I finally made time to see my primary care doctor. For the past three months, I had been bothered by irregular bowel movements and had blood in my stool. When I was referred to a gastroenterologist for further test, I had a foreboding feeling. On December 21, 2017, I had a diagnostic colonoscopy, which revealed "a frond-like/villous and ulcerated partially obstructing large mass . . . in the proximal rectum." Dr. Cohen, who performed the procedure, told me the bad news when I woke up from the anesthesia: "not good . . . surgery is needed . . . when did you have your last colonoscopy . . . they should have caught it." I was cognizant enough to tell him, "I had one in 2008," wondering to myself how this large mass could have grown undetected for nine years! Dr. Hasselle, my radiation oncologist, looked at my CT result later and thought the tumor had been there for at least a year. Did it make me feel better? No. I had trouble processing the news. I thought I had been doing the right thing and taking good care of my health. I'd had reasons to worry. On January 6, 1996, my mother died from diabetes complications, which proved a big wakeup call to me. Ever since her death, I had been monitoring my blood sugar level, eating right and exercising regularly. Who knew I'd trip over my own guts?

But there were things to do, places to go, and people to see. My husband Qiwei and I had planned a trip for the end of 2017 that would take us from Savannah all the way to Dallas, Texas via Alabama, Mississippi, and Louisiana. Not wanting to stay home waiting to die—if you ask me, the diagnosis hit me more like a death sentence—we took off in the afternoon, just a few hours after my colonoscopy. Going in for the procedure, I convinced myself that the worst-case scenario would be hemorrhoids. I could deal with that: Hello, the annoying hemorrhoids. But first I had to deal with the scary diagnosis. Putting on a brave face, I got in the car to start our trip. First stop Atlanta, to our daughter Feifei's house. I had said nothing to her about my visits to the doctors, because I did not want to scare her and ruin her holidays. But more so, I held on to the hope that this was all a mistaken diagnosis, a nightmare I just needed to wake up from.

During the eleven-day trip, we stopped at Birmingham, AL, Jackson, MS, Baton Rouge, LA, Houston, Galveston, San Antonio, Austin, Dallas, TX, Montgomery, AL, Atlanta again on New Year's Eve to ring in 2018 with Feifei and Mike, and finally home to Savannah on New Year's Day. Not a big deal. We executed our plan. We accomplished the goals we set out to, and even squeezed in a few more, like the Waco stop that was nowhere to be found on our initial itinerary.

An avid traveler and photographer, I found it hard to enjoy this trip. A constant whisper rang in my ears: You are going to die, die, die! The weather seemed to echo my feelings. Unusual cold, overcast sky, and high precipitation had swept the entire western part of the country. During the trip, I never felt warm; I hardly saw the sun. I let go of many photo opportunities that I would have seized on in the past. I sat in the car more and more, letting Qiwei explore the world alone. I could not shake off this heaviness in my chest. I kept thinking of the C word. Cancer. How much time do I have? Qiwei and I had plans to travel all fifty states. After this four-state swing, he had visited thirty states plus D.C., and I, thirty-two states plus D.C. Did I have time to visit the remaining states? Just a few more, please! I so looked forward to getting the National Parks Senior Pass so we could visit every national park for the rest of our lives. We were so enamored with the beautiful, majestic, wondrous parks after we visited Acadia in 2015, Arches and Canyonlands in 2016. I had to beat back tears whenever the thought of never going to visit another national park or state came to my mind.

Out of all the places we went to during this trip, San Antonio was the most sentimental. Qiwei and I were supposed to be there in February 2016. Just a day before the trip, he had to rush back to China to be with his ailing mother, who died four days after he got home. I made that trip alone (chaired a panel and delivered a paper at the American Literature Association Symposium. Yea, yea, life goes on). Now almost two years later, when we finally came together to visit this beautiful city, all I could think was how long I had left to live. Qiwei instantly fell in love with the city: "Next time we come, we should stay for a week," he marveled after each photo shoot. "You will have to find a different person to come with you," I said with a straight face, my voice choked a little. "You can always come back with *your* daughter," I added grudgingly. The possibility of not being a part of Feifei's life and leaving Qiwei alone to fend the world was too much to bear. Too gut-wrenching!

The confirmation came while we were in Austin, Texas, touring the State Capitol on December 28. Dr. Cohen was succinct: "Pathologic diagnosis: Rectum . . . Adenocarcinoma . . . will refer you to an oncologist and he will take over your treatment." Just like that, my hope for a mistaken diagnosis was shattered. How on earth I did not collapse then and there in the Capitol, I did not know. Walking back to the Capitol Visitor Parking Garage, I just wanted to sink into the ground, burying all my sorrows and heartaches with me. My blank face, my stiff posture, my lethargic footsteps said it all. Yet, we still had to get to our friends' house in Dallas that evening. Qiwei had driven from San Antonio to Austin in the morning, now he pressed on. About half way, we made an unplanned stop at Waco. I desperately needed to use the restroom while Qiwei needed his caffeine. We found a little café. Sitting across a small table, we drank the freshly ground coffee to warm ourselves up. For a fleeting moment, life seemed to go back to normal. Qiwei, who was never one to take pictures in restaurants or at parties, pointed his smartphone at me. "Smile," he whispered.

So we came back from the trip in one piece. Now, a rare snowfall arrived to welcome the new year. What was in store for me in 2018? Overwhelmed with emotions, I watched the snow falling outside the window, a million thoughts swirled in my head. Would I see snow again? Would I come out of the pending surgery sane and sound? What was my prognosis? Would I lose all my hair? How many more national parks would I get to visit? Would Qiwei, Feifei, and Bleecker, our furry grand baby, miss me and remember me? Would I ever be able to return to the classroom? Would I ever go back to China to see my family and sweep the graves of my parents? I dreaded to know the answers.

Suddenly, something crazy popped in my head. "Go out. Make a snowman! Enjoy this rare weather phenomenon!" I was taken aback for a second. Then, a grin slowly crept across my face. Yay, why not? "Let's make a snowman!" I shouted to Qiwei. Armed with a broom, I stepped out of the door and began vigorously sweeping the snow to a pile. Quickly Qiwei joined in, followed by Bleecker. There was barely an inch of snow on the ground. It did not matter. We scraped the snow with a spade, pushed it with a piece of board, and swept it with the broom, while Bleecker ran around excitedly, leaving his tiny paw prints on the driveway.

In no time, a snowman took shape. Qiwei capped it with his black felt hat, and I strung my red scarf around its neck, red being my favorite color. We took turns taking pictures with the snowman, alone and with Bleecker. Surprised by joy, I laughed for the first time in two weeks. Cancer diagnosis be damned!

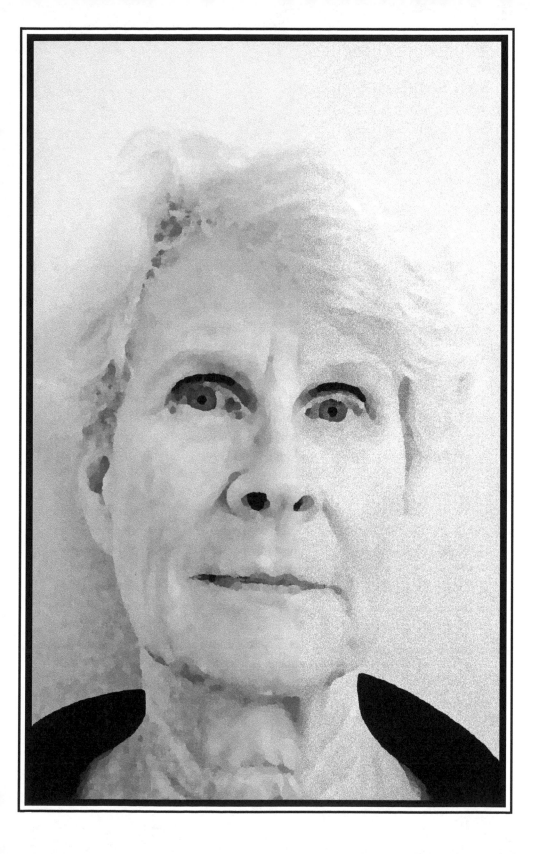

JAN SARCHIO

GRACE IN STAGES

Who can know where thoughts and feelings come from? Why, after a month of feeling lost, separate, afraid and without hope, would I wake up changed? I have thought about God much. I have said that cancer is part of God, as is everything, from a dew drop to a universe. I have known in my head, and in my heart, that I am not ever torn from my source, my Creator. Yet, the doldrums caught me. Maybe because I felt let down by the craziness I see in the world. Maybe because I didn't feel loved or loveable. Maybe because of small things, my birthday forgotten, unkind words, or another bill in the mail. Maybe I was just tired. Maybe it was a phase I needed to go through, so that when I emerged from the tunnel, the light would strike me as so profound, so bright, so wondrous, that I could not doubt my experience.

I went to the doctor on Monday to review a new plan to battle the cancer that has made a home within my body for over seven years. I was afraid of what was to come, how much discomfort the new procedures would produce, and whether they would be of any benefit. Since being diagnosed with cancer, I have rejected the notion of letting it lead my life. I wanted nothing to do with being a victim or being a "Cancer Poster Girl." Little did I realize that its fearful whispers had seduced me, that I had let it in, and let it be in charge of my attitude. To put it another way, I entered the doctor's office filled with cancer. Evidently this change in me was visible, though not yet to me. A nurse, with the desire to be comforting, told me about her brother-in-law who was cured of stage 4 cancer. "He's cancer free," she said, even though stage 4 is believed to be a death sentence. He teetered on the brink, with several perilous cancers attacking his body, but he pulled through. She hugged me and told me to have hope. I had given up on hope and I didn't feel much different after leaving the office.

The next day, my husband, John, and I went out because it was a beautiful cold day and the roads were clear. We just wanted to putter around and do something that didn't involve doctors. We went to the Sagle Thrift Store and I noticed that I was upbeat and back to being my silly self. I kidded with the volunteer behind the desk and I gave a kind word and thumbs up to a young man who had found a pair of jeans and a few shirts. "You found treasures," I said. He smiled, big, and we knew we were lucky. Lucky.

John and I drove back through town. We passed a storefront church that I'd never noticed, perfectly named: Grace Sandpoint. We stopped at the post office, another thrift store and finally the library, where I took the stairs to the second floor. Lately I've been using the elevator, but the stairs looked inviting. I gripped the banister and began the trek upward. My back didn't complain. Lucky. Lucky me. Midway up, the statement that made me begin writing this essay poured into me: "Yesterday, I was full of cancer. Today, I am full of God."

I'm not saying that the cancer went poof, but it wasn't the center of the dance anymore. I was shocked and humbled that I'd let it barge its way into that position. These are sneaky dramas we live through. All I know is I felt effervescent, happy and, well, full of God.

I had, somewhere along the way, forgotten that God is always in charge. God knows the number of days we have been given and when we will be called home. I had become afraid, afraid to go into untold pain, fearful of maybe someday needing to go through this trauma alone. I'd become depressed. I'd begun to believe that was a normal state of affairs, since depression has dogged me on and off since childhood. But, here was this joyful, amazing feeling, filling me. I was, and continue to be as I write this, in a state of grace. Like love, you can't force grace. You can't make people love you; you can't make yourself love anyone. You can choose to be kind, but love is a flood you can't force. Yet for me, yesterday, the man with the new-to-him jeans and the volunteer behind the counter were pals sharing the planet. I gave the woman I passed coming out of the post office a free and easy smile. The overlooked church named Grace became visible . . . How many times had I passed it? A thousand? And the library was suddenly a temple with words not just in books, but in the ether, waiting to enter my heart and remind me, "Yes, yes, I am full of God."

This is healing at the deepest level. Sticks and stones and wayward cells surely can break us. We are, after all, time limited. Much as we gird our loins, grab our bootstraps, put on a happy face and try to be in control, we can only do so much. I was on the verge of giving up. Giving up is not the same as surrender to a higher power. Giving up is doing the backstroke in self pity. It's understandable, but not a good place to hang out. But, lucky us, sweet grace is always here, ready when our timing is right. When the fear of the day is wiped away, grace is there to fill us, to remind us, to lift our weary hearts and deliver joy, absurd as joy might seem.

I am but a small human. I have been in grace many times. I know I am likely to forget again and find myself in the dark tunnel of fear or sorrow or pain. But, I can remember that, like hope, grace is there and again and again it will reassure me, strengthen me, connect me, rejoice with me and help me.

It is hard to tell this story. I know we all understand God in our own way. I am no expert. I have no answers. But, I have gratitude; gratitude, a little golden key. Lucky.

From my heart I say, Thank You dear, everlasting God, for never letting go.

Amen.

HOLY HOLY HOLY

The fine arch of my underarm is like a lost cathedral to me now. Never did I consider my armpit sacred. It never occurred to me to do so. Life must be lived, after all, and there are so many seemingly mundane bits and pieces swirling about, that an armpit, with its wondrous natural curve and the attached musculature, that moves and stretches without a moment's thought, are so innocuous that only when they are torn asunder does one notice how utterly spectacular they were. We come late to so many things and then it is too late to even touch them, for they are utterly and spectacularly gone.

A bi-lateral mastectomy was the terrible wake-up call to this loss. When I stirred from surgery, the deep incisions that traversed my once feminine chest were covered with blood stained gauze. It has been over six years since that life changing day, the day I submitted to a surgery that offered the chance for a few more years, but would give me a body that encumbered as much as it flew.

I have adapted. That is what we humans do. We evolve on a daily basis, whether we notice it or not. My wing-span is no longer fluid. My reach has been greatly reduced, but that is the boring stuff. The truth I wish to speak of is the holy arc of my underarm that once was. Now it is a flat span of flesh. The arch of each sweet arm has vanished due to the pulling and tugging and removal of architecturally necessary body parts: muscle, lymph nodes, cartilage and other things I know nothing of. I never expected the structure of myself to be affected by the "mere" removal of my breasts. Yet, these bits that come together to make this being we find ourselves residing within, are all essential to one another, one resting against the next, so that when a domino falls, much of the adjoining edifice also crumples.

And so it is. Today I sing a song of my fine arching underarms. I sing a song of remembrance and thanks and praise. I miss you, I tell them and in the wee echoes of the ethers, I swear, I hear them sing to me that they miss me too. I love you, I sing. And they, in soft reedy voices, tell me that they love me too. No hard feelings, they tell me. They understand. I tell them that I am sorry for not understanding sooner, and they sigh, for they know of such things. Your toes, they sing to me. Your nose. Your elbows. Your knees. Love, love, love, they sing and I find I am humming. I will remember, I sing, though I know I will also forget. But for now, I sing holy, holy, holy, holy, holy, holy, holy. Grace be unto you.

CHARISSA MENEFEE

JOY

She rushes into bitter water
    Cornish beach in June

Surfers in full-body suits
    the only others there

Sixty-something, on break from
    chemo after two years

Her grandkids shiver, they're
    only up to their knees

She beckons them

Waves crash,
    she disappears

Grandkids rush toward the spot
    where they saw her

She emerges, unsteady, falls
    back into the water and

Laughs
    Laughs
        Laughs

Joy.

DON THACKREY

CANCER PATIENT

Though ill with cancer, I am here outdoors
To walk slow steps and feel the warmth of spring.
By chance, a nearby hermit thrush outpours
His ecstasy to live, to fly, to sing.

And daffodils hurl yellow at the sky
As if they too would venerate this day.
Trees point their buds toward me to testify
That life this time is surely here to stay.

Should this ill man resent spring's revelries
And plead that apt decorum should be due?
No, I will join the season's rhapsodies
And find a way to make myself brand new.

My body may be one grim cancer cell,
But joyful, I will sing "my soul is well."

JANA ZVIBLEMAN

JENNIFER SAID

In life all I've wanted is for someone to fall in love with me.
And when I got the brain tumor I thought
"Well, I guess I won't be getting married."

There's a legacy I've given my girls:
they know how to move a piece of furniture around a corner
on a piece of fabric,
how to make a soup out of bones, get rid of anger,
re-finance a house.

We fixed up these two little houses. I think of downtown as mine. I do.
I take care of it. Sometimes I'm out there sweeping the street.
I love this downtown. Last week, I walked down to get some bread
and I came back with a new guitar.

I've been going on shopping sprees. It's something I never let myself do.
Like I've been buying mustard at the Safeway, for a taste test—I'm a
scientist, you know.
All the mustards. And peanut butter, thirteen kinds, and nine kinds of
horseradish.
Why go through life never knowing which is the best?

Yes, all my African Violets are blooming.
In Oregon—funny.
This is how I take care of them: Don't give them that special food.
It doesn't matter what people say,
don't worry about their leaves getting wet.
You can have one if you want.
I don't need any more plants right now.

I wrote a poem.
How to Fall in Love with a Terminal Cancer Patient.
The poem goes "First: Do ask her how she got the black eye."
So that tells you a lot,
that tells you that the terminal cancer patient
is a female, and that she's not afraid.
She's active, and she's not afraid to go out with a black eye.
and she's still searching for love.

And I did go out. There were times I thought, "Oh, right,
I've got to put the concealer on,"
I would sometimes not bother. My girls would say, "Wear the glasses, they
help cover."
Sometimes I would just not.
After the fall in the Safeway parking lot, the glasses were all bent up.

I don't have any other clues about how to fall in love.

LAUREN K CARLSON

THE WEEK BEFORE
For Noelle

Last week, I stopped by for a visit. Glad to be
home, she smiled under the oxygen tube threaded
through her nose. *Want to hear something stupid?*
She told me a story about trying to twist open
a Gatorade bottle. Not wanting to bother her Brad.
He's done so much. A loud snap at last. But it wasn't
the plastic cap. Her arm instead had shattered.
For dumb. She'd thought. *And now what, the hospital?*
A neighbor came while the children slept.
But doctors managed the pain. Sent her back
home, cancer in every bone. *So, here I am,* she says—
looking at me in the old way. I am holding her hand.
I have never seen someone so beautiful.
The oxygen pump. The hospice bed.
The light coming through the curtain.

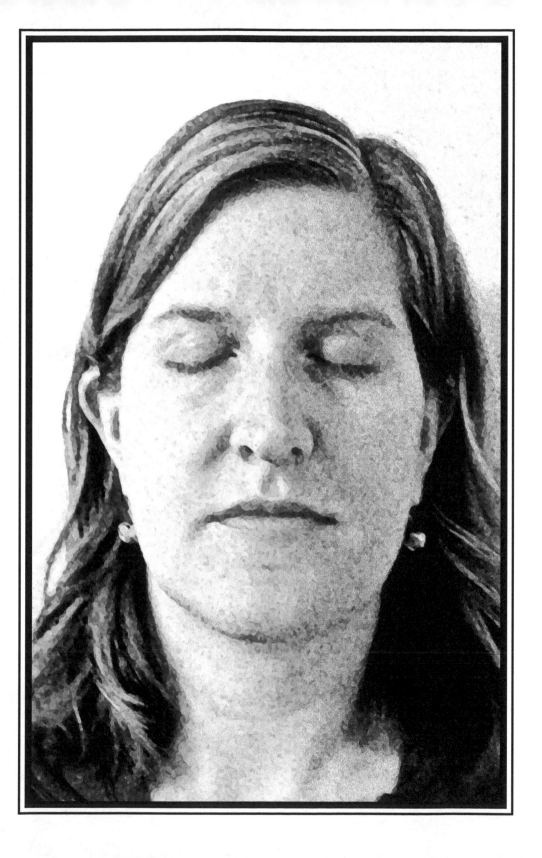

MARK TARALLO

9:45 A.M. AT THE WILLARD HOTEL

Surprisingly quiet.
The Titian-red lobby
feels shy without people,
stillness and silence absorbed by ferns,
chandeliers hanging like fixed teardrops.

A small room through glass:
The private worlds of laps around a table.
A businessman has sleep in his eyes;
another drowses. The silver cream pitcher
gleams like a star.

A painting of an unnamed Victorian woman
in a reverie, worlds away.
She could be in the Duke's mansion,
the archbishop's study.

A well-dressed couple
walks down the long foyer.

I hope my father went to a place like this.
That bed in the middle of the living room,
with the hospice workers who didn't even know him—
that was no place for him.

He deserves marble columns
and the richest of memories,
to be happy and content
in a plush red velvet silence

and,
like the woman in the painting,
still alive somehow.

VIII. NATURE

FELICIA MITCHELL

BY THE CLINCH RIVER, ST. PAUL

I was looking for pawpaws
and found the pawpaws
but there were no pawpaws
so I listened to birds,
some birds I did not know
and some birds I recognized.
By the river, an osprey called,
and then it flew and called again
before it stopped calling.

A coal train came down the tracks
that followed the path of the river
so I paused in my own tracks
and watched it through pawpaw leaves,
this train as loud as electricity.

There were so many pawpaws
and no pawpaws at all,
so I went on down to the falls,
the osprey's call replacing the train's.
When I turned to pick up a walnut,
I found a pawpaw instead.
Carrying my pawpaw back home,
I felt as happy as I know how to be.

Sometimes one is enough.
One hot afternoon, one morel,
one monarch sighting in a season.
One love as biodiverse as a river
where everything you need is there,
even one pawpaw ripe as time.

J. O. HASELHOEF

MANTRAS AND CUKES

At the beginning of the New Year, I adopted a mantra: "Life begins compassionately at the end of my comfort zone." I'd little chance to put it into action when we arrived in Florida mid-January. I spent the first hour of every day stretching and then walking the beach of Panama City—white sugar sand, solid-packed, disappearing into the distant horizon.

On the fifth day of my beach stroll, I saw a sea cucumber:

- Deposited mid-beach by the waves;
- Brown with white spots—plumpy and soft;
- No obnoxious smell;
- It moved slightly in response to a stick poked at it. Still alive; and
- It looked like a slug, but without the antennae—an echinoderm.

Echinoderm or not, I'm no lover of slug-like creatures—whether from land or sea. When I lived in Seattle, I loathed them. Five-inch black slugs appeared on top of the grass after I mowed my lawn. Ten-inch banana slugs suckered up the outside of my tent when I camped. And neon-colored slugs, the size of eighteen-wheeler trucks, populated my nightmares, honking at my little brown sedan on US Highway 5. By the time I left Seattle, I was a mess.

I knew the sea cucumber would die if left on the sand just beyond the reach of the outgoing tide. Perhaps here on Panama City Beach, I could marry my mantra to my actions from which both cucumbers and I would benefit. It would be an empathetic action that saved the lives of the cucumbers and defined the boundary between my ease and discomfort. Each day, I would pick up any sea cucumber I came across and return it to the water.

On my first walk of empathy, I found a total of three of these brown marine creatures. The next day and for most of the days during the next two weeks, a max of five washed in. In the cases where the cuke looked alive (not dried out or shriveled), I grabbed the echinoderm's mid-section with my thumb and forefinger and then, with a wide-arc-movement, tossed it back into the water.   My partner said I might be hurting them as they hit the ocean. I ignored him.

On day thirteen, it was bad for cucumbers. A storm must have churned up the deep sea floor where they crossed on little tube feet, filtering food. Every ten steps along the white-sand beach, there was another one, which I felt obliged to stoop and pick up. It made my walk longer and more tiring than I expected. During the process, I talked to these sluggish animals, "You're a fat one!" or "Back to Mom you go!" or "Brainless, but beautiful!"

Further along the beach, I could see a cluster of seven awaiting my help. I worked to convince myself I could manage the toss of so many at one time without panic. I tried to divert my mind to my words and away from my actions. I said aloud to the first two, "It's just seven from heaven," and to the next four, "Easy peasy, I'm not queasy." Eventually, I lost all composure and screamed as I tossed the last of the seven into the water.

Abandoning my mission came to mind. More than twelve hundred species of sea cucumber exist worldwide. They are not endangered. The Japanese eat them.   Yet they form a small link in the chain of life, offering internal spaces within their bodies to varieties of crabs and worms. They aren't territorial. They communicate to one another by releasing hormones into the water with the intentions of reproducing. And a few medical researchers are looking to sea cucumbers to help with tissue repair, brain scarring, and colon cancer.

I needed a coping mechanism. I wanted a way that I could stick to my mantra without the emotional discomfort. I sat on the beach near to a sea cucumber and considered the situation. I wondered if I stuck my hand into the sand a couple of inches away from its body and scooped the handful up carefully, could I pick up each sea creature on a bed of sand without touching any part of it? I tried. It worked. I solved my problem with sea cucumber sushi.

Re-engaged with my objective, my mantra slid off my tongue easily, "Life begins compassionately at the end of my comfort zone." And as I stooped, scooped, and threw, I repeated, "Life begins compassionately at the end of my comfort zone." I saved 127 sea cucumbers that day.

PEGI DEITZ SHEA

CHARLOTTE'S EGG SAC

Only when the first
raspberries purpled
and I probed the prickers
to reach them, did I see
the pale orb.

A mother spider—
exhausted, invisible—
had laid her egg sac
in the elbow
of stem and branch,
wrapped threads around
a leaf above to canopy
her cradle.

My first instinct:
Extinguish!
Five hundred new spiders
crawling into my home
and laying their own sacs?
The exponential
was exorbitant.

As I clipped the stem,
translucent movement
startled me.
Babies the size
of raspberry seeds
were creeping through

a pinhole and
poking spinnerets
into first air
the way a toddler
dabs at squash.

I called my children.
Pajama'd, barefoot,
they ahhh'd at the sight.
Then together
we carried
the new born
into the woods.

LAURIE KLEIN

HOW TO LIVE LIKE A BACKYARD PSALMIST

Wear shoes with soles like meringue
and pale blue stitching so that
every day, for at least ten minutes,
you feel ten years old.
Befriend what crawls.

Drink rain, hatless, laughing.

Sit on your heels before anything plush
or vaguely kinetic:
hazel-green kneelers of moss
waving their little parcels
of spores, on hair-trigger stems.

Hushed as St. Kevin cradling the egg,
new-laid, in an upturned palm,
tiptoe past a red-winged blackbird's nest.

Ponder the strange,
the charged, the dangerous:
taffeta rustle of cottonwood skirts,
Orion's owl, cruising at dusk,
thunderhead rumble. Bone-deep,
scrimshaw each day's secret.

Now, lighting the sandalwood candle,
gather each strand you recall
and the blue pen, like a needle.
Suture what you can.

LAURENCE SNYDAL

HELIX

My bean vine crawls lazily up its string,
Sprout and spiral, full of life and leaf,
Buoyant and blossoming, it is a thief
Of sun and soil and water. Everything
Joyous spins in a spiral. The fire
Flares up and circles its own core. Matter
Becomes energy. The record platter
Changes its twirling twist into a choir.
Dust devil, whirlpool, waterspout, eddy,
Swirl in their circles. So every spiral
Rises and rotates, becoming viral
Till time turns its stream to steady.
Why spirals form only professors know.
The rest of us are happy and content
To see how energy and force are spent
In circles. We don't care what makes them so,
But marvel at how DNA's deft spin
Can diagram how beans and beings begin.

SUSAN COWGER

THE UNKNOWN LANGUAGE

Sangre de Cristo   Cascades
Granite Peak to Sunlight Basin
Bitterroots and Bighorns
Mountains   I call my angels   my Rocks
Towers of pomp called majesty
Fawned over   as if any one of them
Gives a rip   our imperial assumptions
Always one-sided   I call it
Church of the Missing Door
Where a Piebald eaglet merely waits
For what has been killed to come to him
Seeds melted from resin's captivity
By fire   irresistibly grow and grow
I call yips back to the coyote   and name the black bear
Muggins   hoping for that kind of an in
A charm or goose bump   to signify
I'm with them   and we   are we
From one and the same mind
This sort of reckoning is easy until you try
To get anything from the silence   like if it's true
No one's talking
While all that goodness   echoes off the breastbone

WATCH THIS

Let's call it a drop of water
Hanging on a bare brown branch

You can use that one there
Left by the sprinkler

Or yesterday's drizzle
Please call it yours   for now

Or forget the branch   just wait for the fall
It will fall

And that's it really   but don't worry
This is not just about gravity

Or even the way ablution
Slurs words of confession   though it is

Hard to convey   the gravity of the release
That wink   of free fall

That brief   but perfect sphere
Of mirth   descending

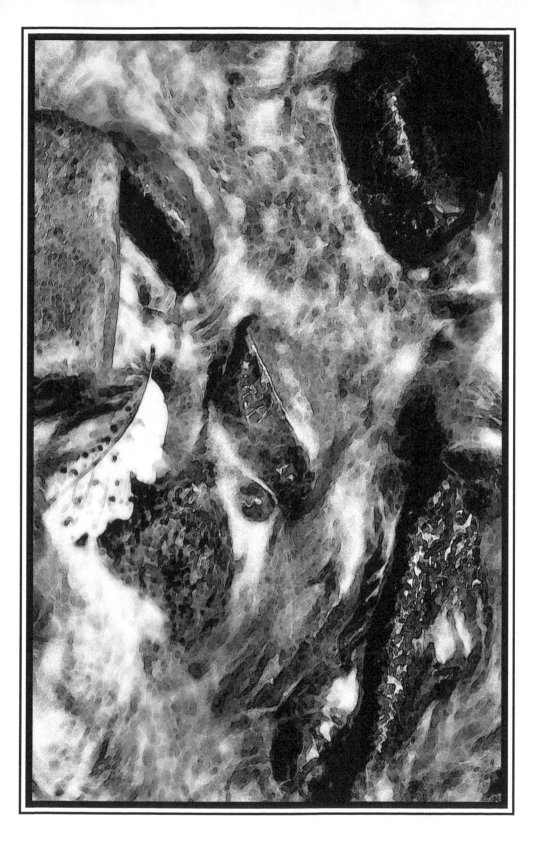

LOWELL JAEGER

CROSSING OVER

A steep climb, lots of strain, a pounding pulse . . .
and now the trail switches back and forth downhill
through alders and hellebore. And blackflies
buzzing my ears. Spring runoff
burbling in the draw yonder

where I plan to bathe
sweat and salt from my shoulders and neck,
splash glacial melt on my sunburnt face.

When I arrive creek-side,
I'll need to ford and find where the footpath continues
somewhere yet unseen. I'll calculate
how to step stone-to-stone and keep dry.

And I'll err as always, failing
to read which exposed river-rocks have anchored
themselves, or which will wobble and falter . . .

as I stumble and laugh aloud, landing knee-deep
in the sobering flow. The chill biting past my boot laces,
soaking socks and blisters, waking in me
an ancient joy: to gasp a last lungful of daylight,
my heart
jolted, my chest aflame
with the radiance of creation,
and the wide, resplendent sky.

KELLY TALBOT

SPREADS HER WINGS

White crane does not want the sky.
White crane does not want.
She breathes in.
She breathes out.
Her body turns.
Her weight shifts.
She sees her fingers extend forward.
As she presses, she feels the air resist.
She stretches, calmly
aware of the power
as it builds within.
Her mind is clear.
Her muscles are relaxed.
She breathes in.
She breathes out.
White crane spreads her wings,
but not to fly.
She spreads her wings
to spread her wings.

IX. ILLUMINATION

MARY KAY RUMMEL

MUSIC FOR A SLEEPLESS NIGHT
Lisbon—in the Alfama

Before she ever moans
from that world edge throat—
rough velvet, cigarette smoke and wine,
the diners begin to clap.

Her bare feet gripping flagstone,
a big woman, neither young nor old,
that voice tangled in long hair
baptized in opaque water.
Dark sounds curl up from her feet,
from below ancient roots.

Something about her childhood
or a broken heart,
Portuguese so close to Spanish
a word now and then floats clear,
her *fados* always sung along this river
erupting from the silence of fish.

Basso profundo—Portuguese music,
voice born from where river meets sea.
She enters you at night,
with her liquid soul possesses you.

VOICES

In honor of Julian of Norwich

Sunrise, crossing the convent garden, she follows
the curve of the path in her usual careful manner
one foot precisely in front of the other,

icy bowl of stale bread in her arms
to feed the famished hens who will rush
at her and fight over crumbs.

Her bare feet ache; she halts dead still,
hears life's eleven thousand reeds blowing
as though mountains and clouds
had found voices—

surely god is also our mother
mother of rust and weed,
mineral-and-yeast-and-rain-and-thyme.

She drops her bowl, lifts her skirts, runs for the trees,
kneels, panting, head bowed
over dark humus, smelling moist green earth.

Disheveled feather dropped by a red finch,
darkest pain unceasing joy
where the spider crouches, waiting for the hoverfly.

* Italicized quotes from Julian of Norwich, The Divine Revelations (14th century), the first book published in English by a woman

LORI LEVY

WATER SHIATSU

He cradles and curls me in the watsu pool
till I'm pressed against his chest, floating
in fetal ease as I follow his lead
and blend with the flow of this dance.
I close my eyes, surrender
to the push and pull of his hands
as he guides and maneuvers my limbs.
He swirls me around, curves and stretches,
molds me into shapes that calm
like the ones I assume moments before sleep.
I am no longer inflexible:
one leg over his shoulder,
the other pointed back in a split—
the image of grace, of poise.
His face is so close to mine
he is breathing with me.
I dip in and out of hearing,
submerging, reemerging.
He seems to be everywhere—behind my head,
beneath my legs, squeezing my waist
between what? His knees? His feet?
Nothing in place, bodies unwinding
as though disconnected,
parts appearing where least expected.
Suddenly I'm tilting, vertical,
feet touching bottom. I open my eyes
and exit the pool: a woman who's been
held and massaged and loosened.
Who carries within her the lapping water.
Who wants to continue the dance.

KRISTIN BRYANT RAJAN

WHAT WE FIND ALONG THE WAY

> *Be patient toward all that is unsolved in your heart and try*
> *to love the questions themselves.—Rilke*

In the cold, quiet hours before dawn,
I feel my way
through the shadows of this house.
The window frames a glow
more bright next to the night
still within these rooms.
A pale half moon is pressed against tender sky
flushed pink in anticipation of morning.
Naked, leaning on the windowsill,
I awaken in this light.

Grateful
to be free
from knowing
the intricacies of lunar cycles,
timed moonrises,
alarms set to mark the random hours of shooting stars.
Free from religious clocks
designating with overarching hands
which stage precedes the other—
as if this journey must always be linear.

Perhaps astronomy and catechism
distract us from the mystery.

Amid constant questioning,
demands for definitions,
the weight of analysis and charted goals,
I stand still.
Unprotected by compasses and scripts,
I awaken in this beauty.

DON THACKREY

BEETHOVEN

Deaf, sour, vain, crude, and mad, with unkempt hair . . .
Those harsh details from his biography
Should not confound us. God gave him a key
To free our souls as if we knelt in prayer
Immersed in grace and heard a deft repair
Of what went wrong, the day's anxiety
Redeemed by chords in healing harmony,
Bright pulsing rhythm, lyric cleansing air.

Note how the music waits in bold ink scrawls:
Stick figures crowding staffs as if a squad
Of angel soldiers, most with flags, spellbound,
Marks time until a baton lifts . . . then falls,
And instruments relay the voice of God
To let the fallen world, for now, be sound.

SILENCE

Speech is of time, silence is of eternity.—Thomas Carlyle

There is a silence that is lack of sound,
As when folks struck with illness cannot hear,
And silence that some casuists hold dear
When trees fall in the woods, no ear around.

There's also silences that can compound
Bruised feelings and combust a spark of fear,
And those that torture eager lovers, sear
Their hearts and bring their soaring hopes to ground.

But there's a silence that is positive,
As when at dawn one stands alone in snow
With all the senses sharpened, cares forgot,
Embraced by peace, rapt and contemplative,
A mystic's mind that's earned the right to know
That silence heard is more than what is not.

J. J. STEINFELD

START BY COUNTING THE GRAINS OF SAND

How much do you need to know
to be free in this life?
Can you embrace freedom
without knowing the names of birds?
Without recognizing the intent of insects?
Without breathing in uncomplicated mysteries?
Can you escape
the doom of the body's treachery
without a mastery of words?
Can you negotiate with God
in silence and with empty pockets?
Can you feast
upon the ordinary and everyday
without touching the lucidity of animals?
The tides, the sunrises, phases of the moon—
can you comprehend without despairing
unknowing and unconcerned?
Storms, absence of storms, sunsets—
can you make calculations of love
inward and hands against ears?

The first question again
repeated as a slap to the senses:
How much do you need to know
to be free in this life?
Start by counting the grains of sand
slowly, one at a time,
overwhelmed by joy.

CLAUDIA VAN GERVEN

A WEAKNESS FOR FALLEN ANGELS

Across a city of desperate steeples
just this scrap of sunshine warming my
shoulder, this gorgeous, poisoned sky, these

small leftover birds singing to the wild
promise of nothing in particular. God
leaps in slow, green light, a mathematical

truth, simple and powerful—so everyday
heaven is always looking for me
with its barbaric, exquisite gaze, till

the winged bones flying up my back
sizzle with a wilder knowing, the way
the words crack open and fly beyond

salvation, toward the fluid geometry
of here and now, with its feathered fears
and outrageous joy. Above the literalness

of life, is the confidence of stars to shine
full of deep mysterious gratitude, time
collapsing into a vast intuitive delight

EVERY ONCE IN A WHILE

God gives up playing dead
just arrives soaked in light and
vertiginous glory. We could simply

fall up to heaven, skies so luminously
blue, so see-through the birds
are Bible pages, speaking gorgeous

nonsense—but we know exactly
what they mean. Flight and swoop—
amazing words to live by. And

all the numbers add up and up
the science of wisdom and the science
of happiness become the unified

theory of joy. Salvation swirls
in the brilliant squawk of black
birds, how they spiral to heaven

in all that holy caterwaul. Divine
encounters make argument
unnecessary, everything said is

in spirit of—"I am that which I
am"—and so are the blackbirds

SINGING IN THE RAIN

that isn't quite music, but a filigreed motion of whispers

playing on your skin, the way the sound slides, a shiver

of silver sequins, as much light as sound and your soul

blossoms—whether you mean it to or not. Suddenly your

cells, the hollows of your bones, are diverse animals alive

with something that doesn't quite make sense, but feels

like a glory of knowing, where thinking is as spirited as

a silver mandala—so intricately simple, the way the rain opens

you up into tender blue blossoms, and you remember you

have skin and hair and nerves—that you are just this

moment—rushing through you, around you beyond you

So that all the crosses on all the churches wink in a new

light and you know God is the song you're singing

HEATHER TOSTESON

ENTRE L'ARBRE ET L'ÉCORCE IL NE FAUT PAS METTRE LE DOIGT

Tch, tch, tching! A song like cracking seeds.
The crows groan in the bare branches. Unh! Unh!
A squirrel scuttles through dry leaves.
In the sky, one long white feathered plume.

A hawk, turning in circles, disappears, glints
back, swoops darkly round, disappears into mist
and flashes back again, bright sliver
of steel, torn metal.

There is a woman here who lost a child last year.
Quietly, she paints, and paints, and paints.
She keeps herself to herself, but when you speak
to her she smiles. She gives directions
to this lake.

The boat house, she has told me, look out
at the lake from there. *Look out.*
Nothing could stop me from stepping into that dark,
damp, reverberant enclosure. *Look out.*
Weeping, tching! tching!

I pause halfway across the slanted floor.
The water drips from the eaves
onto the concrete quais, onto the still brown water.
She knew, did she, what I would find here?
I never want to leave.

Tching! The water dripping from the eaves. Tching!
The branch brushing the water's edge. Tching!
The bird shivering with song. We were meant
to be this way. Secret, quiescent,
open, tching! *Open*

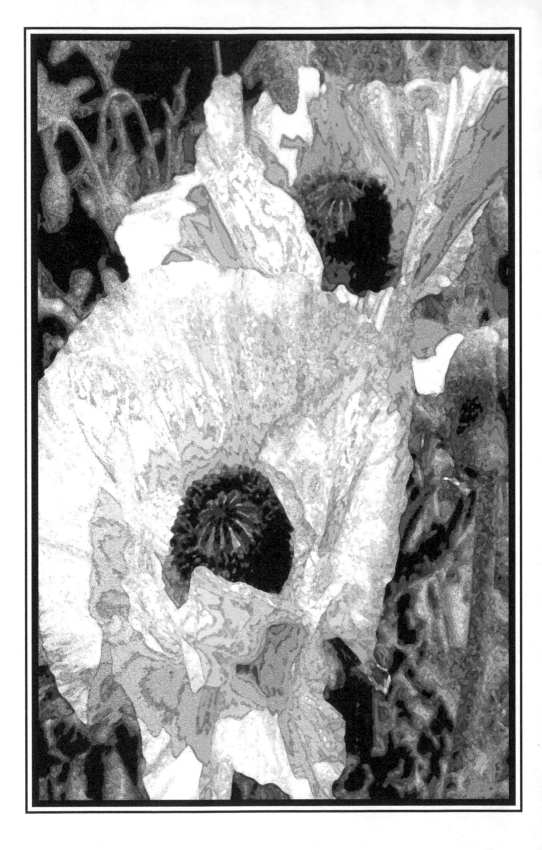

ACKNOWLEDGEMENTS

Lauren K Carlson's "On Mothers Day" first appeared in *Mothers Always Write* (2016).

Joe Cottonwood's "A Gift of Beaches in a Bag" was first published in in *Red River Review* while "Daffodil Madman" was in *Gyroscope*.

Jennifer L. Freed's "Abundance" was first published in *Atlanta Review* (2014) while "Balm" first appeared in *The Healing Muse* (2017).

Margaret Hasse's "Day after Daylights" appeared in *Between Us*, "What the Window Washers Did" in *Earth's Appetite*, and "Water Sign" in *Milk Tides,* each published by Nodin Press.

Lowell Jaeger's "Genesis," "Wondrous World," and "Crossing Over" were previously published in *Earth-blood & Star-shine* (Shabda Press, 2018).

Daniel Jaffe's "The Kiss" previously appeared in *Nightfire* (2011) and his *Jewish Gentle and Other Stories of Gay-Jewish Living* (Lethe Press, 2011).

Laurie Klein previously published "From The Cuckoo Clockroom" in *Relief* and "How To Live Like A Backyard Psalmist" in *Where The Sky Opens.*

Kerry Langan's "My Name Is Your Name" appears in her collection *My Name Is Your Name & Other Stories* (Wising Up Press, 2017).

Felicia Mitchell first published "Bourrée with Goldfinch" in *Young Ravens Literary Review.*

Zack Rogow previously published "Sunday Morning Bernal Heights" and "French Quarter" in *The Selfsame Planet* (Mayapple Press, 2000): "Eager for Each Detail" and "Learning to Be Happy" in *Make It Last* (Slow Motion Press, 1983); and each also appears, along with "A Little Before 3 p.m.," in *My Mother and the Ceiling Dancers* (Kattywompus Press, 2011).

Alison Stone's "Who Would've Thought" previously appeared in *Dangerous Enough* (Presa Press, 2014) and "Bird" in *Dazzle* (Jacar Press, 2018).

J. J. Steinfeld's "Start By Counting the Grains of Sand" was first published in *Writes of Freedom* (The Ontario Poetry Society, 2004) and in a slightly different version in his *An Affection for Precipices* (Serengeti Press, 2006).

Kelly Talbot previously published "The First American" in *Lullwater*, "Impact" in *Pacific Review*, and "Spreads Her Wings" in *Stone Voices*.

Don Thackrey's "Beethoven" previously appeared in *Trinacria* (2010), "Cancer Patient" in *First Things* (2014), "Silence" in *The Eclectic Muse* (2010) and each is included, along with "My Winter Son," in his *Making a Prairie: A Verse Journal from the Nebraska Sandhills* (2015).

Heather Tosteson's "Entre L'Arbre et L'Écorce, Il Ne Faut Pas Mettre le Doigt" was first published in *Zone3* and collected in *The Sanctity of the Moment: Poems from Four Decades* (Wising Up Press, 2015). "We Are All Donors Here" was published earlier in *Germs of Truth* (Wising Up Press, 2013). She created the photographs in this anthology.

Rosemary Volz previously published "Wonder" in *Love & Other Passions*.

CONTRIBUTORS

Patricia Barone's new collection of poetry is forthcoming from Blue Light Press, which previously published her *The Scent of Water*. Her *The Wind (fiction)* and *Handmade Paper (both* New Rivers Press) each received Minnesota Voices awards. Other awards include a Loft-McKnight Award of Distinction in poetry, a Lake Superior Contemporary Writers Award, and a Minnesota State Arts Board Career Opportunity Grant.

Zan Bockes, a direct descendent of Bacchus, the Roman god of wine and revelry, earned an MFA in creative writing from the University of Montana. Her work appears in numerous publications and she has had four Pushcart Prize nominations. Her first poetry collection, *Caught in Passing*, was released in 2013. Another collection, *Alibi for Stolen Light,* is forthcoming in 2018.

Lauren K Carlson is a poet and writer, mother and wife, living in rural Dawson, MN. She has published her poetry in *Tinderbox Poetry Journal, The Windhover, Mothers Always Write, Heron Tree* and *Blue Heron Review* among others. In addition to poetry, she also spends her time as a spiritual director and teaching artist.

Joe Cottonwood is a carpenter by day, writer by night—self-taught in each. His most recent book is *Foggy Dog: Poems of the Pacific Coast.*

Susan Cowger's chapbook, *Scarab Hiding,* was released in 2006 by Finishing Line Press. Most recent work appeared in CRUX, *Poem-a Week (AllWeCanHold.com* Sage Hill Press), *McGuffin,* and *The 55 Project.* She is founder and past editor of *Rock & Sling: A Journal of Witness.*

Margaret DeRitter is the copy editor and poetry editor of *Encore* magazine in Kalamazoo, MI. She worked full time as a journalist for thiry years and has taught journalism at Kalamazoo College and Western Michigan University. Her poetry has appeared in *New Verse News, The 3288 Review, Third Wednesday, Pocket Change, Midnight Circus, Melancholy Hyperbole, Scarlet Literary Magazine* and *Encore.*

Joan Dobbie, MFA, teaches poetry and yoga, and co-hosts the River Road Reading Series in Eugene, OR. Find her poetry in journals and anthologies including Wising Up's *Love After 70* and most recently, "Mildred" (Red Sofa Poets, 2017) as well as her collection *Woodstock Baby: A Novel in Poetry* (2014).

Terri Elders, LCSW, a lifelong writer and editor, has contributed to over a hundred anthologies, including multiple editions of *Chicken Soup for the Soul.* She writes feature articles and travel pieces for regional, national, and international publications. After a quarter-century odyssey, including a decade overseas with Peace Corps, she recently returned to her native California.

Jennifer L. Freed's poetry appears in journals and anthologies including *Zone 3; Atlanta Review; Connecticut River Review; Forgotten Women, a Tribute in Poetry* (Grayson Books, 2017); and *Aftermath, Explorations of Loss and Grief* (Radix Media, 2018). Her chapbook, *These Hands Still Holding,* was a finalist in the 2013 New Women's Voices Competition. She has twice been nominated for a Pushcart prize.

Andrew Paul Grell is the author of *Scapegoats,* a Biblical science fiction novel, as well as *Calm of the East River* (American Writers Review) and assorted contributions to the *New York Times*. He is an "accidental writer" concentrating on environmental solutions informed by religious ethics. He lives in Manhattan with his wife, Melody, and the puppy. By day he uses mathematical modeling to detect fraud.

Patrick Cabello Hansel has published poems, stories and essays in over 45 journals, including *Crannog, Ilanot Review, Hawai'i Pacific Review, Ash & Bones, Switchback, RiverSedge* and *Lunch Ticket.* An award winner from the Loft Literary Center and the MN State Arts Board, his poetry collection, *The Devouring Land,* will be published by *Main Street Rag* in 2018

Andrea Hansell studied creative writing at Princeton University and earned a PhD in clinical psychology from the University of Michigan. She was a practicing psychotherapist for many years and is now a consultant and scriptwriter for Glowmedia mental health education films. Her essays and short stories have appeared in publications including *Lilith, Intima, DaCunha Global, Lascaux Review* and *Easy Street.*

Linda Hansell is a writer and educator who has published essays in *The Emerald Coast Review* and *Months to Years,* and has co-authored two books of biography, *Dancing in the Wonder for 102 Years* and *Memories of a Life.* She holds a PhD in education from the University of Pennsylvania and BA from Williams College.

J. O. Haselhoef is a social artist who writes and travels. Her work appeared in print or online at *Fiction Southeast, Milwaukee Journal Sentinel, Extra Newsfeed, Healthcare in America, Haiti Global,* and *Stuff dot Life.*

Margaret Hasse lives a few hundred miles from the source of the Mississippi River. *Between Us,* her most recent collection of poetry, received the Midwest Independent Publishing Association's 2017 poetry prize. Hasse's poems have been stamped on sidewalks and displayed as posters on public transportation in Minnesota's Twin Cities metropolitan area.

Lowell Jaeger, Montana Poet Laureate 2017–2019, teaches creative writing at Flathead Valley Community College in Kalispell, MT. He is author of eight collections of poems, founding editor of Many Voices Press, graduate of the Iowa Writer's Workshop, winner of the Grolier Poetry Peace Prize, and recipient of fellowships from the National Endowment for the Arts and the Montana Arts Council.

Daniel M. Jaffe is author of the novels *Yeled Tov* and *The Limits of Pleasure;* the novel-in-stories, *The Genealogy of Understanding;* and the short story collection, *Jewish Gentle and Other Stories of Gay-Jewish Living.*

Laurie Klein has published poems in *The Southern Review, The Pedestal, New Letters, Barrow Street, Terrain,* and other journals and anthologies. A past winner of the Thomas Merton Prize for Poetry of the Sacred, she is the author of a poetry collection, *Where the Sky Opens,* and a chapbook, *Bodies of Water, Bodies of Flesh.*

Kerry Langan has published dozens of stories in literary journals, magazines, and anthologies and is the author of three books of short fiction, all published by Wising Up Press: *Only Beautiful & Other Stories, Live Your Life & Other Stories,* and *My Name Is Your Name & Other Stories.* She was also a co-editor of Wising Up Press anthologies, *Shifting Balance Sheets: Women's Stories of Naturalized Citizenship and Cultural Attachment, Creativity and Constraint,* and *Siblings: Our First Macrocosm.*

Lori Levy's poems have appeared in *Poet Lore, Poetry East, RATTLE, Nimrod,* and numerous other literary journals and anthologies in the U.S., England, and Israel. One of her poems was read on a program for BBC Radio 4. She grew up in Vermont, lived in Israel for sixteen years, and now lives with her family in Los Angeles.

Charissa Menefee is a poet, playwright, director, and performer. Her chapbook, *When I Stopped Counting,* is available from Finishing Line Press, and her poetry can also be found in *Adanna, Poetry South, Terrene, Poets Reading the News, The Paddock Review, Twyckenham Notes,* and Telepoem Booths. She teaches in the MFA Program in Creative Writing & Environment at Iowa State University.

Felicia Mitchell, a native of South Carolina, has made her home in southwest Virginia since 1987, with poems growing from her relationships with the earth and with family. Her recent collection is *Waltzing with Horses* (Press 53). An essay is included in *Connected: What Remains As We All Change* (Wising Up Press).

Kristin Bryant Rajan has a PhD in English, with a focus on Virginia Woolf, and an interest in the nature of identity in modernist literature. She is a lecturer in English at Kennesaw State University and enjoys writing fiction, poetry, creative non-fiction as well as literary criticism. She finds writing to open her awareness to the wonders of each day.

Zack Rogow is the author, editor, or translator of twenty books or plays. His eighth book of poems, *Talking with the Radio,* was published by Kattywompus Press. The most recent of his series of plays about authors, *Colette Uncensored,* had its first staged reading at the Kennedy Center in Washington DC in 2015 and ran for six months at The Marsh in San Francisco and Berkeley in 2016-17 and in London in 2018. He is a contributing editor of *Catamaran Literary Reader.*

Mary Kay Rummel was Poet Laureate of Ventura County, CA for 2014-2016. Her eighth book of poetry, *Cypher Garden*, was recently released by Blue Light Press. *The Lifeline Trembles* won the 2014 Blue Light Award. New work appears in the anthologies, *Bright Light* (Bright Hill Press) and *Carrying the Branch: Poets in Search of Peace* (Glass Lyre Press).

Frank Salvidio, a 2014 Nemerov finalist whose poetry has appeared in various journals and anthologies, is also the author of *Between Troy & Florence* (poems and translations) and translations of Sappho (*Sappho Says*) and Dante (both the *Vita Nuova* and the *Inferno*). His most recent book is *Inventing Love*, a sonnet sequence.

Terry Sanville lives in San Luis Obispo, CA with his artist-poet wife (his in-house editor), and two plump cats (his in-house critics). Since 2005, his short stories have been accepted by more than 280 literary and popular journals, magazines, and anthologies including *The Potomac Review*, *The Bitter Oleander*, and *Shenandoah*. Terry is also an accomplished jazz and blues guitarist.

Jan Sarchio, a west coaster, has lived in North Idaho for the past twenty-five years. *Northern Journeys* and several regional publications have printed many of her short stories, essays and poems. Jan has been known to sculpt, paint and refinish furniture that needs attention. She's made many gardens and planted lots of trees. She's married to her best pal, John.

Deborah A. Schmedemann spent over three decades as a law professor, writing textbooks on legal research and writing. She completed the Master Track Program in Creative Nonfiction at the Loft Literary Center in Minneapolis and published *Thorns and Roses: Lawyers Tell Their Pro Bono Stories* (2010). She is working on a collection of essays for Luke inspired by Keith's life.

Pegi Deitz Shea, award-winning author of sixteen children's books, has also published more than 400 poems, articles and essays for adult readers. Her exhibit, "Through a Poet's Eye: Photographs and Poems," is currently touring in Connecticut. Her poems have recently appeared in journals including *Earth's Daughters*, *bottlerockets*, *here*, and in the anthologies *Forgotten Women*, *The Kindness of Strangers*, and *Cardinal House*.

Ruth Margolin Silin, former director of development at a pediatric hospital and assistant to her daughter in her clothing boutique, now spends time writing more poetry and taking classes at her retirement community on the campus of a local college in Newton, MA. Her poems have appeared in many journals and anthologies and focus on themes of love, loss and diversities of life.

Laurence Snydal is a poet, musician and retired teacher. He has published more than a hundred poems in magazines such as *Caperock*, *Spillway*, *Columbia* and *Steam Ticket*. His work has also appeared in many anthologies including *Visiting Frost*, *The Poets Grimm* and *The Years Best Fantasy and Horror*. Some of his poems have been performed in Baltimore and NYC.

J. J. Steinfeld, a Canadian writer, has published eighteen books, including *Would You Hide Me?* (stories, Gaspereau Press, 2003), *Misshapenness* (poetry, Ekstasis Editions, 2009), *An Unauthorized Biography of Being* (stories, Ekstasis Editions, 2016), and *Absurdity, Woe Is Me, Glory Be* (poetry, Guernica Editions, 2017). Over fifty of his one-act plays and a handful of full-length plays have been performed in Canada and the United States.

Alison Stone published four collections: *Dazzle* (Jacar Press, 2018), *Ordinary Magic* (NYQ Books, 2016), *Dangerous Enough* (Presa Press, 2014), and *They Sing at Midnight* (recipient of Many Mountains Moving Poetry Award, 2003). Her poems appeared in *The Paris Review*, *Poetry*, *Ploughshares*, and others. She was awarded *Poetry*'s Frederick Bock Prize and *New York Quarterly*'s Madeline Sadin Award. She's a licensed psychotherapist.

Kelly Talbot has edited books for more than twenty years for Wiley, Macmillan, Pearson Education, Oxford, O'Reilly, and Microsoft. His writing has appeared in dozens of magazines and anthologies. Kelly divides his time between Indianapolis, IN, and Timisoara, Romania. He also practices yoga and taijiquan, most recently focusing on the "White Crane Spreads His Wings" sequence.

Mark Tarallo is a writer based in Washington, DC. His poetry and fiction have appeared in *Abbey*, *Asphodel*, *Angel Face*, *Beltway*, *Innisfree Poetry Journal*, *Manorborn*, *Red Mountain Review*, *The Best of Vine Leaves Literary*

Journal, and the Wising Up Press anthologies *Cold Shoulders, Evil Eyes* and *CONNECTED: What Remains As We All Change.*

Don Thackrey has been writing and publishing formal verse since 2007. He was fortunate to have published his book *Making a Prairie: A Verse Journal from the Nebraska Sandhills* in 2015 shortly before having a major stroke curtailing much of what he formerly loved to do. Nevertheless, he continues to be surprised by the joy of love, music, silence, and life.

Claudia Van Gerven has been published in a number of magazines and journals, including *Mom Egg Review, Calyx, Prairie Schooner, The George Town Review,* and many others. Her poetry has won several national awards. She resides in Boulder, CO, where she has taught English Literature and Writing.

Rosemary Volz has had her short stories published in *Blueline, Event* and *Another Chicago Magazine.* Her poetry has appeared in *Evening St. Review, Reader's Choice, Earth's Daughter,* Write Wing Publishing, Conversations Across Borders, Wising Up Press, *Baseball Bard, Hospital Drive, Nebo, Pinyon, Third Wednesday, River Run Journal* and *Feile-Festa.* She now lives in Ponce Inlet, FL and has twice won the Flagler County Poetry Award. She is currently associated with the Tomoka Poets and the Dan Pels Poetry Salon.

Kenneth Wise's short story "Sledding" was published in the anthology *Uncertain Promise.* He lives in Fairfax, VA with his wife and two children.

Weihua Zhang is a published writer and photographer. In her book *Dream Variations: A Journey Across Two Continents* (2012), Zhang presents a candid account of one Chinese American woman's journey across two continents. Zhang teaches at The Savannah College of Art and Design in Savannah, GA.

Jana Zvibleman, Poet Laureate of her own backyard in Oregon, has collaborated with sculptors, painters, buskers, and flugelhornists. Also a visual-artist-on-the-loose, her focus ranges from humor to out-and-out grief, from real to fictionish. Her first stage play premiered in 2017. Her work appears in the finest publications; her story "Bucket of Water" is in the Wising Up anthology *The Kindness of Strangers.*

EDITORS/PUBLISHERS

CHARLES BROCKETT has a PhD from UNC-Chapel Hill and is a recipient of several Fulbright and National Endowment for the Humanities awards. A retired political science professor, he has written two well-received books on Central America and numerous social science journal articles and book chapters. With Heather Tosteson, he is co-founder of Universal Table and Wising Up Press and co-editor of the Wising Up Anthologies.

HEATHER TOSTESON is the author of seven books of fiction, poetry and non-fiction, including most recently the novel *The Philosophical Transactions of Maria van Leeuwenhoek, Antoni's Dochter.* She holds an MFA in Creative Writing (UNC-Greensboro), a PhD in English and Creative Writing (Ohio University), and Diploma in Spiritual Direction (San Francisco Theological Seminary) and has received creative fellowships in writing and photography from MacDowell, Yaddo, Hambidge, and the Virginia Center for the Arts.

Visit our website and learn about our other Wising Up Press publications, readers guides, and calls for submissions.

www.universaltable.org
wisingup@universaltable.org

P.O. Box 2122
Decatur, GA 30031-2122

CPSIA information can be obtained
at www.ICGtesting.com
Printed in the USA
FFHW02n1834010818
47598060-51104FF